Crimson and Gold

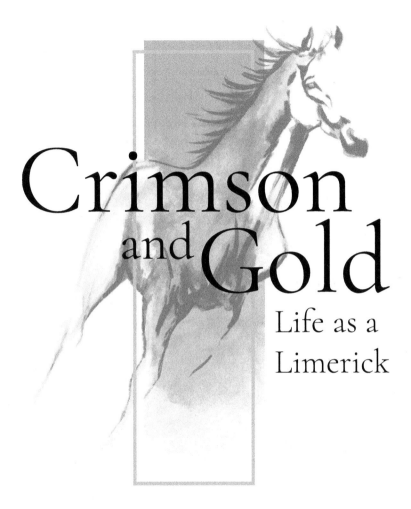

Crimson
and Gold

Life as a
Limerick

MARK PATRICK
HEDERMAN

columba
BOOKS

First published in 2021 by

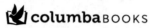 columbaBOOKS

Block 3b, Bracken Business Park,
Bracken Road, Sandyford, Dublin 18, D18 K277
www.columbabooks.com

The author/editor and publisher gratefully acknowledge the permission
granted to reproduce the copyright material in this book. Every effort
has been made to trace copyright holders and to obtain their permission for the use of copyright material. The publisher apologizes for any
errors or omissions and would be grateful if notified of any corrections
that should be incorporated in future reprints or editions of this book.

ISBN: 978-1-78218-379-2

Set in Adobe Garamond Pro 11/15
Cover and book design by Alba Esteban | Columba Books
Printed by ScandBook, Fallun

For Fanny Howe,
who taught us to write,
by letting it rip.

CONTENTS

I

Climbing the Hill of Truth

'This is why Moses was warned when he was about to build the tabernacle: "See to it that you make everything according to the pattern shown to you on the mountain."'
(Hebrews 8:5)

Knockfierna

In sight of the Galtee Mountains - a thirty kilometre range in the counties of Tipperary and Limerick in Ireland - between the River Deel and the river Maigue, a ridge of old red sandstone rises abruptly from the limestone land of the surrounding area. *Cnoc Fírinne* (Hill of Truth) is almost 1,000 feet high. It has a cairn on top, a large heap of stones added to it by those who climb the hill on pilgrimage. This cairn is called *an buachaill bréagach* [the deceitful boy]. Near the cairn is an opening known as *Poll na Bruíne,* an entrance to the underworld. The word *Brú* occurs in the names of towns in the locality, Bruree and Bruff for instance. It refers to such underground hostels as are found at the great megalithic site in the Boyne valley called *Brú na Bóinne.* Knockfierna is the palace of Donn Fíreannach, god of the dead and of fertility. He rides on horseback.

A cross-country hurling match between the *Slua Sí* of *Cnoc Fírinne* led by Donn and the *Slua Sí* of Lough Gur and *Cnoc Áine* (Knockainey) led by the goddess Áine takes place every Autumn. The ball is thrown in half-way: fifteen miles between Knockfierna and Knockainey. If Donn drives it back to Knockfierna the crops will thrive; if Áine gets the upper hand, the people of Ballingarry will have to look out for themselves.

My mother was American. She came from Boston to study at Trinity College, Dublin for a degree in Arts. Invited for a weekend to a farm in County Limerick, my father fell in love with her as she was getting out of the car. He was the youngest of four boys and one girl, whose father owned a stud farm. Realising that Josephine Mullaney was only staying the weekend, John Hederman plucked up his courage and asked her to marry him.

'I know absolutely nothing about you,' mother protested.

'You know as much about me now as you're ever going to know,' my father replied, 'so, you'd better make up your mind.'

I was born, their second child, on the 18th June, 1944, in a nursing home in Hatch Street, Dublin. The doctor said he could hear me from the street outside the hospital as he came to work, my protests were so loud. My older brother had been called John, one of the traditional family names, such as Daniel, William, Patrick, Joseph, Anthony. My father was John as had been generations of his predecessors. Having submitted to family protocol on the first occasion, my mother insisted on naming her second child. 'How is it, she asked, that Daniel, William, Patrick, Joseph, Anthony, all end up as Dan, Bill, Pat, Joe, and Tony?' 'With an ugly name like Hederman,' she continued, 'you need a first name of one syllable.' The choice she gave them was Karl or Mark. In 1944, naming someone 'Karl' was like calling him 'Heil' to rhyme with Hitler. Mark it was.

Innishfree

I didn't realise at the time what a privilege was mine to be born into the most perfect Catholic country since the Acts of the Apostles. There are moments in history when destiny calls and certain countries get their opportunity to reinvent themselves: America with the Declaration of Independence in 1776, France after their Revolution in 1798, Russia after 1917. Ireland, having shuffled off the yoke of serfdom, reinvented herself during the first half of the twentieth century. Having defined what it meant to be human, she then set in place the most perfect socio-political and economic structures ever before seen in the universe.

Dr James Devane, writing in the *Irish Rosary* in 1952, suggested that 'the Republic of Ireland, as it is constituted today, is the only integral Catholic state in the world; a Catholic culture as it existed in the Middle Ages'.[1] Ninety-three per cent of our population were practicing Roman Catholics. And what did that mean practically speaking? It meant weekly (often daily) attendance at Mass, regular processions, pilgrimages, confraternities, sodalities, parish missions, benediction, novenas, the rosary, Marian devotions, the Nine First Fridays, cults of devotion to saints, a picture of the Sacred Heart plus the eternal lamp in every home, the Papal Marriage Blessing on the wall, the St Martin de Porres 'Black Babies' box in every pub and every shop, with the Catholic Truth Society stall at the back of every church, to give orthodox guidance to the faithful on all the thorny issues of the day.[2] If Rome were to give out rosettes for the most Catholic country in Europe during the first half of the twentieth century, Ireland would have won the red as outright winner; Franco's Spain might have come second, and Salazar's Portugal a close third.

Of course no one would dream of suggesting that the Irish Free State was a theocracy but one could say that this country in the 1950s was Catholicism 'effectively transformed into a civil theology'.[3] 'During the first fifty years of independence, leaders of both Church and State, irrespective of political allegiance, shared a desire to develop the country according to a philosophy of Catholic nationalism.'[4]

In 1948, when I was four, the Taoiseach of our country, John A. Costello sent a message to Pope Pius XII assuring him, in the name of his

1   Louise Fuller (2005) Religion, politics and socio-cultural change in twentieth century Ireland, *The European Legacy*, 10:1, 41-54, DOI: 10.1080/1084877052000321976.
2   Ibid.
3   D.V. Twomey, *The End of Irish Catholicism?* Dublin, Veritas, 2003, p. 33.
4   Daithí Ó Corráin, *The Cambridge History of Ireland, Volume IV, 1880 to the Present,* Cambridge University Press, 2018, p. 733.

cabinet colleagues, of their 'filial loyalty' and 'firm resolve to be guided in all [their] work by the teaching of Christ and to strive for the attainment of a social order based on Christian principles'. Many Irish politicians saw themselves as Catholics first and legislators second. The impression of Ireland held in Rome in the early 1950s was of a country which had preserved a purity of faith in the face of persecution and famine, a country loyal to Rome, in which the combined might of the apparatus of Church and State was exercised in keeping at bay the kind of modern influences, which were perceived as undermining the Christian heritage.[5]

On the 10th April, 1951, a letter was received by the Secretary of the Congress of Irish Unions from Monsignor Montini, Substitute Papal Secretary of State and future Pope Paul VI, acknowledging the address of homage and the chasuble presented to Pope Pius XII during the Holy Year in the name of the workers of Ireland. The letter, as recorded in the *Irish Catholic Directory* in 1952, reads as follows:

> At a time when so many of the workers of various countries have fallen prey to false theories and ideologies that are in direct contrast to the Christian religion, it was a source of particular gratification to His Holiness to receive this further proof of the devoted attachment of the workers of Ireland to the Vicar of Christ, and to their fidelity to the Catholic Faith, which is their nation's most precious heritage.

In 1937 the so-called De Valera Constitution of our 'free state,' expressed this derived philosophy in no uncertain terms. In a radio broadcast to the United States on 15th June that same year, De Valera called it 'the spiritual and cultural embodiment of the Irish people' and to mark its first anniversary in 1938, he reminded us: 'As faith without good works is dead, so must we expect our Constitution to be if we are

5   Louise Fuller, (2005) Religion, politics and socio-cultural change in twentieth-century Ireland, The European Legacy, 10:1, 41-54, DOI: 10.1080/1084877052000321976

content to leave it merely as an idle statement of principles in which we profess belief but have not the will to put into practice.'

So, the pudding had set, you might say, in the 1950s. The Catholic Church and its clergy and bishops up until the 1960s, and perhaps beyond, exercised and enjoyed an influence without parallel in Europe.[6]

Such a cherished reputation required much hard work, supervision and discipline. Obsessed by a constant threat to Catholic purity, from foreign, especially English, influences, something akin to moral panic swept through the newly formed Irish Free State. It was not just the Church and the State, but also Catholic lay groups who led the charge and became unofficial guardians of our national purity. A motion was proposed at a meeting of the Wexford Bee-Keepers Association in 1932 that George Bernard Shaw be expelled. This unworthy, who had unwittingly become an honorary member on inheriting property in the area from his uncle, was accused of making 'observations that struck with sarcastic ridicule at the very foundations of Christianity'.[7] By 1945 the organisation called Maria Duce was vociferous in its supervision of public morality. The League of Decency, a body with similar objectives had *The Rose Tatoo* by Tennessee Williams closed down at The Pike Theatre in Dublin in 1957 and its director, Alan Simpson, imprisoned for 'producing for gain an indecent and profane performance'. In September that same year, the Taoiseach Éamon de Valera received a letter from the Irish League of Decency requesting an interview:

> 'This letter is written as a despairing cry from a frustrated body of Catholics to clean-up on indecent books, picture-post cards, films etc ... we have done almost all we can — we are still storming heaven — within the law to combat the imported press and film evils, but are being thwarted by the very law itself and so find ourselves foiled

---

6 Thomas Bartlett, The Cambridge History of Ireland, Volume IV, 1880 to the Present, Cambridge University Press, 2018, p xxxiii.

7 Peter Gahan, from an unpublished manuscript shown to me by the author.

to remove sources of scandal from public display ... where are we? Where do we go from here? We must and will carry on the fight ... Mr De Valera, for our dear Lady's sake at least grant us an interview that we may show you some of the stuff being sold in Catholic Ireland—it's even going the round in the classroom.'[8]

Two and a half years later *The Ginger Man* by J.P. Donleavy was closed after three performances at the Gaiety Theatre because of indecent and obscene references which the author refused to cut.

Ireland represented itself both to itself and to the world as a light to the nations, a light-house off the coast of Europe, a zealous missionary for the angelic nature of humanity. Sean O'Faolain described De Valera's philosophy as 'something so dismal that beside it the Trappist Rule of Mount Melleray is a Babylonian orgy'.

Both the Church and certain institutions sanctioned by the government were committed to warding off the constant threat to Catholic purity from foreign influences. American movies, 'the Harlotry of Hollywood,' became enemy number one. James Montgomery, the official in charge of film censorship, made it clear: 'one of the greatest dangers of ... films is not the Anglicisation of Ireland, but its Los Angelesization.'

Magazines dating from the 1920s such as *Our Boys*, were launched for the specific purpose of 'maintaining the National Virtue of our Country'. Such campaigns held puritanical views about sex on the one hand, and belief in the racial superiority of the Irish in terms of sexual morality on the other. These ideologies won a major victory in the Censorship of Publications Act of 1929.

By 1943, the year before I was born, over 2,000 books had been banned in Ireland, including some writings of Saul Bellow, William Faulkner, Graham Greene, Robert Graves, Ernest Hemingway, Christopher Isherwood, Alberto Moravia, Nabokov, Proust, Jean-Paul Sartre, Dylan

---

8   History Ireland, Vol. 18, Jan/Feb, 2010.

Thomas, H.G. Wells and Emile Zola, to provide an alphabetical sample of the international fare. Irish authors from Liam O'Flaherty in the 1930s to Lee Dunne in the 1970s received the same treatment. Such Irish authors included Frank O'Connor, the two Nobel prize winners, Beckett and Shaw, Austin Clarke, and both Kate and Edna O'Brien. It was said at the time that many an Irish writer took it as a slur on their reputation as artists if their works had not been banned.

Books could be considered a cool medium to use McLuhan's helpful distinction, in the sense that you had to be able to read to get the message. The newly established film industry was decidedly 'hot'. Kevin Rockett, in his study of Irish Film Censorship, calls the cinema an 'engulfing aesthetic'. The darkened amphitheatre with its sumptuous upholstery allowed consumers to be sucked in and swallowed up by an all-engulfing strange new world. The Censorship of Films Act in 1923 provided for the appointment of an Official Film Censor and a nine-person unpaid Censorship of Films Appeal Board.

James Montgomery and Richard Hayes held the office between them for more than 30 years. As the first appointed, James Montgomery set the tone for those coming after him. Guided by theological certainty, he set out a strict moral blueprint that lasted for half the twentieth century. Next came Richard Hayes, who was a medical doctor and a friend of de Valera; growing up with him in Bruree, Co. Limerick. These appointed film censors tried to 're-edit' the Hollywood narrative to conform to the ideals of Irish society. Of course, the difficulty with 'motion pictures' is the 'in your face' moving image. Once actors and actresses began to move on the screen there was little hope of censoring their gyrations. When Marilyn Monroe, Marlon Brando or Brigitte Bardot move on the silver screen, before they ever open their mouths, sexuality invades the space around them. Charles Laughton put it famously in 1935: 'They can't censor the glint in my eye.' Movement inevitably led towards dancing and Irish censors had a particular aversion to dancing. The can-can, the rhumba, the boogie-woogie, and above all the jitterbug were cut out of every film. A documentary about *Fishing in Hawaii* had two shots removed for Irish viewers as they featured a hula dance.

Some of our early statesmen were aware of this underhand power of cinema. During a Dáil debate on the Censorship of Films Bill in the early 1920s, William Magennis - Professor of Metaphysics at University College Dublin and Cumann na nGaedheal TD - expounded at some length on the evils thereof:

> Purity of mind and sanity of outlook upon life were long ago regarded as characteristic of our people. The loose views and the vile lowering of values that belong to other races and other peoples are being forced upon our people through the popularity of the cinematograph.

Magennis was worried about the effect that cinema would have even on those chosen representatives who would guard the rest of us from obscenity. For him, cinema was equivalent to a deadly plague, what Ebola might represent today. The normal ordinary person did not have the defences required for viewing films. Only medical doctors, who had built up immunity through their work in combating disease ... would be capable of dealing with the pestilence of cinema ... and while his advice was not strictly followed, it is true that doctors (medical and psychiatric) have featured prominently among Ireland's Official Film Censors, all of whom have been men. Five of these officially appointed censors spanned the fifty years between 1923 and 1972.

The Catholic hierarchy worried about 'occasions of sin' embedded in many new-fangled entertainments. Unseemly movement was not confined to the silver screen to which not every parishioner had access. Nearer home, springing up like mushrooms all over the country were local dance-halls.

'Company keeping under the stars of night had succeeded in too many places to the good old Irish custom of visiting, chatting and story-telling from one house to another, with the rosary to bring all home in due time', an archbishop chided his flock in 1926. A year later, in 1927, the bishops of Ireland issued a joint pastoral in which they pointed out:

> The evil one is forever setting his snares for unwary feet. At the moment, his traps for the innocent are chiefly the dance-hall, the bad book, the indecent paper, the motion picture, the immodest fashion in female dress - all of which tend to destroy the characteristic virtues of our race.

Despite the view that Irish teenagers were different from the rest of the world, Bill Haley's *Rock around the Clock*, and all the later Elvis Presley films of the 1960s, got Irish youth dancing and rioting in the cinema aisles exactly like teenagers everywhere else. Screened in Sligo, for example, in November 1956, extra Gardaí had to be drafted in to deal with 'mass hysteria'. Councillor J. Dolan of Sligo Corporation described them as 'hysterical nit-wits in drain-pipe trousers copying what they had seen across the channel'. It wasn't us, it was alien 'others' who were forcing this upon us. Left to ourselves we would have been immobile paragons of Irish purity.

The twentieth century with all its technological innovation and cultural fashions became the dragon pitted against the wilting flower of Irish purity.

Just when the censors felt they had begun to get a grip on films entering the country they were faced with an even greater pandemic: the television. Every home in the country could have a traitor in the sitting-room spewing out foreign filth in every direction. A situation even more impossible to supervise where 40% of the population were exposed to 'spill-over signals' from British and Northern Ireland TV channels by the end of the 1950s. When ITV opened in 1956, the censors were of the opinion that this channel was 'governed by ideas wholly alien to the ordinary Irish home'.

It is true that all over Europe after The Great War a fear of moral degeneracy was prevalent. But, in Ireland, the new Republic was particularly single-minded and fanatical about establishing its own national dugout. John McGahern puts it succinctly: 'When I was in my 20s it did occur to me that there was something perverted about an attitude that thought that killing somebody was a minor offence compared to kissing somebody.'

Ballyneale

The confusing thing for someone on a stud farm in County Limerick was that this was not the Ireland they were born into, or the one they had experience of growing up. My father's family came from Knockfierna. Their house, 'The Glen,' had a castellated wall jutting out from the side which, I am told, was a sign to Cromwell's troops to leave it untouched. Why the castellated wall and why this gentling effect on the destroyers, remain a mystery.

Massacres and confiscation of property were the norm for troops led by Cromwell in 1653. The landed gentry of Ireland had been changed from Irish and Old English (Anglo-Irish) to Protestant New English in a very short time. Lands in the provinces of Leinster, Munster and Ulster were given to veterans of the Parliamentary Army and adventurers under Cromwell and Ireton. For any dispossessed incumbents who would accept transplantation, properties were reserved in the province of Connacht, excluding coastal lands and most of Counties Sligo and Leitrim. 'To hell or to Connaught' became the despairing slogan.

Following the collapse of the Cromwellian regime in December 1659, a period of uncertainty ensued. The policies of Charles II in Ireland resulted in further land settlement during the 1660s. When the Roman Catholic James II ascended the throne in 1685, a more pro-Catholic policy was enacted. However, three years later, when James was removed, the Irish prepared to rebel and invited the ousted King to lead them. James borrowed troops from France and landed in Ireland in 1689, the year that William (III) and Mary ascended the throne in England. In June, 1690 William landed at Carrickfergus to face the Jacobite forces and the Irish. The English defeated James on the banks of the Boyne on 11th July, 1690. James fled to France to his benefactor, Louis XIV.

The war ended with the Treaty of Limerick in 1691. The terms of this Treaty were seen as fairly satisfactory to the Irish, but were subsequently dishonoured and Limerick became known as the city of the violated treaty.

In 1695 penal legislation enacted against the Irish Catholics and Dissenters meant that until 1728 Irish Catholics were prevented from practicing their faith and the majority of wealthy Catholics were stripped of their estates.

Our family was Catholic at a time when Penal Laws ostensibly forbade Catholics to own property, even a horse worth more than five pounds. And yet, the Hederman family owned land under Knockfierna. A tombstone in Shanavoha graveyard, above Granagh church, registers the burial of John Hederman who died aged 71 in 1784. This primeval 'John' must therefore have been born in 1713.

How or why the family were protected during these Penal times remains an unsolved mystery. The name is unusual. It sounds German and some might associate it with the Palatines who came from Germany to settle in Limerick in the early eighteenth century. Not so. The Palatines were Protestant. Our name comes from the Irish Ó hEadroman, meaning lightfooted. It is first found in the barony of Moyarta, County Clare, where family tradition holds that bearers of the name were ferrymen for St Senan.

All of this is to explain that my grandfather, Daniel Hederman, born in a house called 'The Glen' under Knockfierna, was a Catholic in County Limerick who owned a stud farm and a thousand acres, was one of the first Catholic Magistrates elected in West Limerick, and was the first Barony High Constable for the county. All of which qualified him to be recognised as 'gentry'. This term is defined in reputable dictionaries as 'well-born, genteel and well-bred people' of high social standing; families of long descent who might never have obtained the official right to bear a coat of arms, or even if they were armigerous (having a coat of arms, dummy), did not have titles of nobility. This group represented Irish landowners, and those aspiring to this status from among the merchant and professional community. There you go.

When my grandfather distributed his lands between two of his four sons, my father inherited Ballyneale Stud, while my uncle Vincent, his older brother, lived with his wife Eileen at The Glen under Knockfierna.

Ballyneale is an early nineteenth century late-Georgian period house with flanking wings. It has two storeys over a basement, and was built by the Cox family who had a corresponding house and property across the road in Ballinamoe. This other older house is now a derelict ruin and barely stands as a grim reminder of what might have happened to ours. But, *au contraire*, ours went from strength to strength, grandeur to grandeur. Over the last forty years it has had at least ten major facelifts. The first owner, after we left in 1968, installed central heating by placing a boiler in the basement which sent shockwaves throughout the fabric of the building, accustomed to the temperature of an arctic igloo. As a result the lintels of the doorways and the frames of the windows shrank, so that each had to be replaced with some compatible material. This eyelid surgery or blepharoplasty cost three times the amount originally paid for the house.

In 1979, ten years later, Ballyneale was featured as 'house of the month' in *Image* magazine. Here we were told that it had been restored extensively by an American interior decorator in a way that was 'garish and lacklustre'. This insensitive restoration necessitated yet another complete overhaul.

Whatever about the inside, the outside and surroundings with a view of Knockfierna to the North and the Galtee Mountains to the South, remain more or less as they always were. Coming back through these fields on a horse-drawn hay-float at evening time, I remember thinking to myself that there could be no more beautiful place in the world.

In 1990, I happened to be sitting with Lew Glucksman [Wall St. financier] at a fundraising dinner in New York. Making conversation, he told me he had bought a property in Ireland. I asked him where, and he said he wouldn't even try to explain it was so remote and so difficult of access. Eventually we came to realise that he and his wife Loretta were now living in my old home at Ballyneale.

But the house has changed hands even since then.

'€8 million is not a trifling sum,' says a report in the *Irish Times* in 2013, 'and, yes, maybe you could buy the Massif Central, all the apartments in some dreary east German city, or, the entire Republic of Montenegro for the same price - but in the through-the-looking-glass world of Irish property prices, Ballyneale House is a steal.' The present owners, David and Ros Pearl have poured 'torrents of money' into a no-expenses-spared upgrading. Their ideas of improvement include 'a private golf course; a grass landing strip for light aircraft; a luxurious, air-conditioned cinema; a billiard room; an all-weather tennis court; a heated outdoor swimming pool'.

When I come across it now in magazines and newspapers, I hardly believe that I spent my childhood in this palatial residence. A child doesn't question or negotiate the circumstances of his or her disembarkation on earth. Mine was particularly fortuitous but I only became aware of this much later. Nor do I have any sense of nostalgia or regret; just sheer amazement: like finding out that your nanny was, in reality, the Dowager Empress of Manchuria in disguise.

My father, John Hederman (1907-1984), was the youngest in a family of five. His dearest wish was to join the British army. Although he himself was a Catholic, most of his friends in County Limerick were Protestant, many of them fighting in World War II. He was prevented from joining them by my grandfather who feared for the safety of his house and property. Many such 'big houses' were burnt down by freedom fighters who saw them as remnants of colonial bondage. Any attempt to aid the British was regarded as treachery by those determined to secure independence for Ireland. England's difficulty being Ireland's opportunity, we were supposed to remain neutral in the war between the Allies and Nazi Germany.

There can be no doubt that the Ireland I was born into was quite different from what was advertised on the package. I did not go to school until I was nine. My American mother believed that children should not go to school until they themselves asked to do so. As she had a university degree, she could follow this principle without breaking the law. So the first nine years of my life were spent roaming the hillsides of West Limerick, with my sister Louise, mostly on horseback. The edge of our farm abutted a roadway leading directly to Knockfierna. We spent most of our days riding in the vicinity of this sacred hillside.

West Limerick is a place of high ringfort density south of the Shannon estuary. There was a ring fort on a forty acre field at the east edge of our own stud farm. There is another at Ballingarry Down on the approach to Knockfierna. I spent much time in both these ringforts. Although it has been suggested that they were occupied from the Bronze Age (1,800 BC) more recent dendrochronology and radiocarbon dating suggest a period between 600 and 900 CE for their construction. Whatever about their chronology, these were openings to another world. I later discovered that all cultures, and most children, all around the world, are aware of this alternative dimension. Anthills in Africa serve a similar purpose.

Knockfierna is the palace of Donn Fíreannach, God of the Dead. An old man who worked for my father told me he heard 'fairy' music on his way back from the church in Granagh. As he looked through the low open window of his room out on Knockfierna, he knew that he would be there soon on the whale-backed Black Hill beside it.

My first understanding of the presence of God is linked with this mountainside. It was here, before I was nine years old, that I swore allegiance to the one true Deity on 'the hill of truth'. Later when I began to study theology I found that my teachers had little interest in Donn Fíreannach or his *buachaill bréagach*. They regarded all that as nonsense at the best of times and heresy at the worst of times. Pagans and Heathens, I later learned, were those who lived in the countryside (*paganus*) and dwelt on the heath. As so many before me, I went into hiding like Heathcliff, and became, as Jacob and Ulysses, a deceitful boy.

When I first went to school after nine years of heath dwelling, my religion encountered its first turbulence. Very few of the other children had any direct connection with God. The school organised an annual retreat to facilitate such encounter and I was amazed at how unsuccessful these introductions proved to be. On one occasion when I was ten years old, a particularly dreary attempt to engage was being made by Fr Gabriel Harty, the famous Rosary priest of Ireland, who died in 2019 at the age of ninety eight. He would have been in his early thirties at the time, and was already a well-known and established preacher. How had he been persuaded to spread his erudite instruction before a yawning bunch of ten-year-olds? I understood the imbalance. After his first talk I went to his room and told him that he wasn't getting through to these people at all. If he would let me replace him at his next talk I would tell them all about God in a way they might understand. He was very kind and told me that his next talk was going to involve a series of slides about Our Lady's appearances at Lourdes and that I could help him by manning the slide projector. I was disappointed for both of us. I knew he had thrown away the opportunity of a lifetime.

Not everyone was quite as tolerant of my claims to affiliation with the Divine. In the early 1950s, I was handed my guide book to correct living in the Ireland of my time: *A Catechism of Catholic Doctrine*. Published by Gill and Son in 1951, approved by the archbishops and bishops of Ireland and with an *imprimatur* from no less an authority than John Charles McQuaid, it was the creation of Maynooth. It answered every question you might think of from 'Who made the world?' to 'How should we prepare for extreme unction?' No need to worry our little heads about existentialism or other diseases afflicting the rest of the world, we had our *Vade Mecum* which was compulsory teaching in all Irish Catholic primary schools, where children were required to memorise each question and each answer by rote. Teachers in the school, armed with different kinds of sceptres or croziers beat out heresy and converted pagans. A local priest with a bamboo cane beat the answers of the Catechism into those who were slow or uninterested. I knew all the questions with their answers by rote and still do. They had very little, if anything, to do with my conversations on Knockfierna.

Blackbird and Bell

The first half of the twentieth century was a battle for the 'soul' of Ireland. The Roman Catholic Church, as the century progressed, became the highest and the loudest bidder. This battle for the citadel became polarised into two camps, those defending a Gaelic nationalism and those promoting a cosmopolitan internationalism. Since most of the *intelligentsia* were Protestant, it turned into a war between cultures. Spokespersons from each side, like AE and Shaw[9] on the one hand, and leading politicians - who publicly vaunted in contrast that they were not intellectuals - on the other, presented almost contrary opposite views of the architecture of the new nation-state.

Shaw called for the abandonment of nationalism saying that it must be added 'to the refuse pile of superstitions'. Anyone who wanted to divide the race into 'elect Irishmen' and 'reprobate foreign devils (especially Englishmen) had better go and live on the Blaskets where he can admire himself without much disturbance'.

The Irish language was going to be a way of cutting off influence from outside, according to AE, who was afraid it was being used as 'a dyke behind which every kind of parochialism could shelter'. He wanted 'world culture, world ideas, world science; otherwise Ireland would not be a nation but a parish'. He used *The Irish Statesman*, founded in 1923, as a vehicle. 'The cultural implications of the words *Sinn Fein* are evil', he wrote in 1925, 'We are not enough for ourselves. No race is. All learn from each other. All give to each other. We must not be afraid of world thought or world science. They will give vitality to our own nationality. If we shut the door against their entrance we shall perish intellectually, just as if we shut the door against the Gaelic we shall perish nationally.'

Others, like W. B. Yeats, set out to represent an alternative spiritual tradition. He believed that one of his tasks was to provide his country and, indeed, the world, with the elements of a more vibrant religious life.

....

9   Writers George William Russell and George Bernard Shaw (Ed.).

He wrote in his introduction to Lady Gregory's *Gods and Fighting Men* (1904): 'Children at play, at being great and wonderful people' are the true reality of what we are and what we should become. Mankind as a whole had a like dream once; everybody and nobody built up the dream bit by bit and the storytellers are there to make us remember.' But the children of the twentieth century had put away these ambitions 'for one reason or another before they grew into ordinary men and women'. Yeats dated our defection to the seventeenth century. 'What Whitehead calls "the three provincial centuries" are over. Wisdom and Poetry return.' The twentieth century was meant to be the privileged time of reawakening.

The wisdom which Yeats believed to be our most precious heritage can only be expressed through poetry. The word of God can never be relayed through prose. If this means that the message is sometimes obscure that is not because the poet is being deliberately obscurantist, it is because we are moving in a borderland area for which ordinary language is not designed. There is a religion which reneges on its responsibility to discover such Truth and which becomes a search for immunity against the shocks of life. Such a fearful attempt to hide from the demands of human passion and human life is, for Yeats, a denial of the two essential mysteries of Christianity: Creation and Incarnation. Such an impoverished religion was the one being proposed, in Yeats's view, for the new Ireland of the twentieth century.

According to Elizabeth Butler Cullingford, 'Yeats also knew that his name had become a byword for paganism, anti-Catholicism, opposition to Gaelic culture, and snobbery'.[10] The Catholic culture being supported and diffused by *The Catholic Bulletin* described the Nobel Prize which Yeats won in 1923 as 'the substantial sum provided by a deceased anti-Christian manufacturer of dynamite'. 'It is common knowledge,' the report continued, 'that the line of recipients of the Nobel prize shows that a reputation for Paganism in thought and word is a very considerable

....

10   Elizabeth Butler Cullingford, *Gender and History in Yeats's Love Poetry*, Cambridge, 1993, p. 144.

advantage in the sordid annual race for money, engineered, as it always is, by clubs, coteries, salons and cliques.'[11]

Roy Foster's biography[12] shows the persistence and depth of antagonism between Catholic Ireland, as incarnated in the newly established Free State and the 'New Ascendancy' 'epitomised by people like Yeats, Gogarty, Plunkett and Russell, and entrenched in institutions such as the Royal Irish Academy, Trinity College, and the Senate'.

> Swear by those horsemen, by those women,
> Complexion and form prove superhuman,
> That pale, long visaged company
> That airs an immortality
> Completeness of their passions won;
> Now they ride the wintry dawn
> Where Ben Bulben sets the scene.

> Here's the gist of what they mean.

> Irish poets learn your trade
> Sing whatever is well made,
> Scorn the sort now growing up
> All out of shape from toe to top,
> Their unremembering hearts and heads
> Base-born products of base beds.
> Sing the peasantry, and then
> Hard-riding country gentlemen,
> The holiness of monks, and after
> Porter-drinkers' randy laughter;
> Sing the lords and ladies gay

11 Foster, II (2003) p. 256.
12 R.F. Foster, *W.B. Yeats: A Life*, I: The Apprentice Mage 1865-1914, Oxford University Press, 1997; II: The Arch-Poet, 2003.

That were beaten into the clay
Through seven heroic centuries;
Cast your mind on other days
That we in coming days may be
Still the indomitable Irishry.

Cast a cold eye
On life, on death.
Horseman, pass by![13]

13   W.B. Yeats, 'Under Ben Bulben,' *Last Poems*. 1939.

II

Life with the Limericks

Life with 'The Limericks' for most of my father's friends meant foxhunting. The people in charge were Protestant. They had created for themselves a world of pageantry and excitement which gave meaning to their lives and filled their days. Perhaps they were escaping from a post-war Labour government in Britain and living in ways which would have been impossible under similar circumstances in the England of that time. They were an elite but not a clique. They invited any who lived around them, with the same interests, to join in the fray as spectators or as participants. If you owned or could borrow a horse or a pony, you were one of the 'Limericks'.

Dorothy Reynolds ran the pony club where children were taught the lore and protocol of horse riding. If a fox was killed during your first hunt you were 'blooded' as into some ancient tribe; boys were presented with 'the mask,' girls with 'the brush' as those in the know called the head and the tail of the totem animal. Mrs Murray ran the annual gymkhana at her home in Ballynochane, Ballingarry. Gymkhana, as everyone in Ballingarry was expected to know, came from the Persian word 'Jamat-khana,' which during the British Raj described social or sporting gatherings in the Indian sub-continent.

The person around whom this farrago revolved was a much revered Master of the Limerick foxhounds, Toby Daresbury. His father, Sir Gilbert Greenal of Cheshire, was created Baron Daresbury in 1927. The family had been involved in brewing from the mid-eighteenth century and had thereby accumulated sufficient wealth to become what envious scoffers called 'beer peers'. In 1938, Toby, the second son, became the second Baron: Edward (Toby) Greenall (Lord Daresbury) (1902-1990).

Toby Daresbury was what Joxer Daly would call 'a darling man'. He had been Master of the Belvoir Hunt (pronounced 'Beaver,' of course) in Leicestershire, a role he shared with the Duke of Rutland. When he retired, he bought Clonshire and Mount Coote in County Limerick where he became Master of the hounds for thirty years from 1947 to 1977. Toby did not merely enjoy foxhunting; it was his lifelong passion. He brought with him to Ireland hounds from the Belvoir pack to breed his own branch for the Limerick hunt.

His first wife died in a hunting accident and after his second wife died in 1958, he married in 1966 the celebrated hunting personality Lady Helena Hilton-Greene, who had followed him to Ireland. Known to all her friends as 'Boodley,' she was the daughter of Earl Fitzwilliam and the former wife of 'Chetty' Hilton-Greene of Cottesmore. Stunningly beautiful, she looked her magnificent best in hunting gear mostly of dark green. She was greatly disapproved of by the parish priest of Ballingarry, Canon Thomas Wall (PP 1936-1956), for whom she was something of a Jezebel to his (self-appointed) Elijah. She was a blotch on the canvas being painted in his territory of Ireland as the Colleen Bawn or Eileen Aroon. There is an account of Cearúil Ó Dálaigh (composer of *Eilín a Rún)* travelling to Kilmallock to get Eilín to elope with him: he noticed a white horse going up the hill of *Cnoc Fírinne*. He followed it to the *Poll Dubh* where he found a horse grazing but no sign of its rider. He threw a stone down the *Poll na Bruíne*. It was thrown back hitting him in the face and breaking his nose.

Canon Wall was an Irish nationalist to the core. His *Little World of Don Camillo* pitted him, as parish priest, against the English invaders, epitomised and personalised in the hunting élite. He would now and then threaten boycotts of all foxhunting in his parish unless the relationship between Toby and Boodley were satisfactorily regularised. Toby and Boodley paid as much attention to him and his successor, Archdeacon Canon Lyons, as they would to the deer that sometimes threatened the spoor of their hounds, trained meticulously to follow only the scent of a fox.

There were the two Catholic parish priests in Ballingarry while Toby was master of hounds. Archdeacon Patrick Lyons was appointed in 1956 after Canon Wall's twenty year reign. Patrick Lyons lived to be 106. He died in 1999 as the oldest priest in Ireland at the time. When he was a hundred he celebrated his birthday with a big party in the parish hall at Ballingarry. Many of the local Protestants joined their Catholic neighbours to wish the doughty patriarch 'God speed' in whichever direction. The Archdeacon gave a speech on the occasion at the end of which he said that he only had two enemies during his long lifetime, not a lot for someone of his age he hoped that all present might agree: these two enemies were the British and the Protestants. An embarrassed but understanding shuffle identified the newer more tolerant generation in the room.

Boodley was as passionate about hunting as Toby and both were nearly always seen on horseback. She brought with her to Limerick her daughter from her first marriage, Julia. They became mythological figures in this fairytale world. Once kicking off her riding boots at the Dunraven Arms hotel in Adare, Boodley caught her foot in the radiator which came away from the wall and smashed her ankle. The plaster was cast in a way that allowed her to carry on hunting. In 1970 she died from a fall while out hunting with the Limericks. When my mother asked Toby what it was about Boodley that so attracted him, he said it was her hair.

Merry Atkinson was another of Toby's devotees. Daughter of a doctor in the same Belvoir Country in Leicestershire, she also followed Toby to Ireland and became one of this whippers-in. Her real name was Meriel. She was completely dedicated to this world of fox hunting, and was highly successful at breeding and rearing both horses and hounds. Diminutive of stature, she had a huge heart, a loud voice, and nerves of steel. After a fall from her horse during one of the hunts she climbed onto a wall and shouted in her deep-throated voice: 'pony, pony, pony!' Her home-bred horse, which had gone careering after the hounds, turned back and collected her from the side of the wall. Every hound was known to her personally. She had been midwife to each one and knew them by name. She could stop the whole pack in full flight by shouting in the same imperious voice: 'puppy, puppy, puppy ...' They would obediently grind to a halt.

The puppies were fostered out to farms in the county to be raised as pets for the first years of their existence. Each was named in alphabetical order to identify their pedigree and the litter from which they were born. We would have two each year at Ballyneale and they were adorable pets. Fed only on oatmeal, they were allowed no meat until they tasted the fox who was to become their prey. When they were mature enough to return to Clonshire we would be as broken-hearted as they were. We would visit them at the kennels as if visiting a child at boarding school. On the first occasion they would be visibly homesick, recognise us immediately, and beg to be taken 'home' in the car. Some weeks later, after they too had been 'blooded' they hardly recognised anyone. They had become entirely monogamous and the fox had become what Lacan[14] might term their '*petit objet a*', their irreplaceable and unattainable object of desire.

Nor were they the only ones thus infatuated. All over Limerick were scattered those whose life was focussed on foxhunting. Marjorie Waller was old and blind but nothing would persuade her to take up a less life-threatening hobby. She wore spectacles like telescopes and rode side-saddle. People in front of her would shout 'Duck to your left, Marjorie,' when there was an overhanging branch above the bank she was about to jump. Often she was left suspended from the branch as she got hooked and the horse moved on. She could be found urging her steed to plunge into the River Maigue which she had mistaken for a double-bank. Her butler, James, following around in the car, would pick her up in a field crawling on her hands and knees towards her horse grazing nonchalantly ahead of her as in a portrait by Stubbs.

Another spectacular huntaholic was Tony Bullock. He was paralysed on one side of his whole body and had to be hoisted onto his horse each morning of the hunt. Sometimes the hoister misfired and Tony would career over the saddle and land on the ground on the other side.

....

14   French psychoanalyst and psychiatrist Jacques Lacan (Ed.).

Undaunted, he would settle himself eventually into the saddle and hack his way to the meet, always trotting along the middle of the road, heedless of traffic behind or before. He stayed in the saddle until evening when he would reluctantly return home. In his will he left instructions that his body was to be fed to the hounds so that he might enjoy one more day's hunting in the belly of a hound.

Such an expensive pastime demanded finance and personnel. Young people interested in riding, and in furthering a career around horses, would come as stable boys and stable girls from all over the world. They did Trojan work for little pay. One such was Patricia Rosemary Smythe (1928–1996), more commonly known as Pat Smythe. She came as a stable hand to the Hutton-Wilsons who had no idea that she would later become, it is said, the world's most successful woman showjumper. As an unknown stable hand with the Limerick hunt she was given no favours or preference. Rugged conditions, minimal food, no free time, such minions as she were expected to sacrifice everything for the privilege of being undercarriage to the great enterprise. And, indeed, their employers and superiors were no less ascetic; living like Spartans they sacrificed all to the thrill of the 'view halloo'. 'Among my most enjoyable days,' Pat Smythe recounts, 'was when we rode to the hill of the fairies – the celebrated landmark called Knockfierna, whose summit, they said, was haunted.'

To the amazement of all, she went on to win the Bronze medal in the Team Jumping event at the Olympic Games in Stockholm in 1956. She wrote her autobiography *Jump for Joy* in 1954. In it she had the temerity to describe the harrowing days she spent as stable girl in County Limerick. Bed bugs where she stayed with the Hutton Wilsons were only the beginning. She likened one stalwart of the hunt, Peg Watt of Riversfield, to a toby jug.[15] After much consultation, Peg decided to

---

15   A toby jug, also sometimes known as a Fillpot (or Philpot), is a pottery jug in the form of a seated person, or the head of a recognisable person. Typically the seated figure is a fat, heavy-set, jovial character holding a mug of beer and wearing eighteenth-century attire: a long coat and tricorn hat forms a pouring spout, often with a removable lid, and a handle which is attached to its rear.

assume in her person all the seething outrage of the county, first of all because Pat Smythe had become so famous, and then for daring to make mention of the Limerick hunt in anything but glowing terms. Wattie, as Peg was called behind her back by both friend and foe, would represent us all by taking an action against the author for libel. After some straight talking and serious discussion with lawyers, she was advised that unless she could prove that she didn't look like a toby jug the case, in light of immediate and incontrovertible evidence to the contrary, would be dismissed. She hadn't a leg to stand on.

It was not until 1970 that Toby took on his first joint master, Mr A. R. Tarry. 'We came over here soon after Mary and I got married. I was 26 and she was 21. We had to go somewhere to escape her interfering father and it came down to a choice between my being a vet in Fiji or in Ireland. We chose Ireland and we are very pleased we did. My father bought the rectory for us with all the furniture; he bought the original cars, too. I was an only child.'[16]

It was the father's dream to see his only son riding on horseback in the striking livery of a Master of Fox Hound. The hunt needed money and such would be the bargain. The only trouble was that although Tony was passionate about hunting, he wasn't so keen on the rough and tumble involved. 'Hunting was an addiction for me. I used to say I'd give away the last ten years of my life if I could go hunting. Looking back now I can't understand it. Even if it was a very bad meet and you knew you wouldn't get out of a walk, I still wanted to go.'[17] If truth be told, he seemed much happier with 'a very bad meet'. He would ride his horse along the road while the hunt itself went careering through the countryside. As always there would be large groups of local people standing on ditches along the road watching the spectacle. Forty or so horses chasing as many hounds across the fields is an eye-catching sight. Tony wasn't quite sure where the

....

16 *Life among the spoilt few Tony Tarry remembers his arrival in Co. Limerick in 1952.* A conversation with Amber Sinclair and Sue McSwiney Islanmore, Croom, 17 June 2009.

17 Ibid.

hunt was and he shouted at the viewers on the ditch: 'I say there, have the gentry passed by?' 'Indeed they have Sir,' came the wry reply: 'about two hundred years ago.'

Although children under seventeen were not required to dress formally, everyone else wore specific hunting gear. The Master wore a dashing read coat which everyone referred to as 'pink'. The reason for this is not clear. Explanations ranged from 'worn and seasoned attire dulled by so many days of ardent service to the cause' being more fashionable than bright clean gleaming, brand-new apparel to the existence of a famous and fashionable tailor whose name was Pinke. Whatever the derivation, these scarlet coats gave vivid focus to the autumnal palette of the fox hunt pageantry as sometimes even eighty horses preceded by as many foxhounds galloped across the picturesque Limerick countryside.

The 'Gentry,' where not ennobled, used their rank in the army (British, of course) to establish their perch on the ladder of precedence: Brigadier-General Rupert Brazier-Creagh of Tarbrook in Croom towered over Colonel Dicky Langford from the Old Rectory; he ranked higher than Major Hopes-Helis, living as far away as Mallow. If on a shoot, when the troops arrived at a bog, you shot in this order of your rank. There was one woman among all the men, Elsie Hunt. She was the most accomplished angler and a crack shot, downing snipe and woodcock with a left and a right where the men watched their prey flying off unscathed. 'Knocked a hatfull of feathers out of 'em' was the pathetic cry from the bunglers. Each of your dogs had to be perfectly trained. As Dad's Army crept forward to surround the snipe bog and puffed their way to the planned positions of attack, an untrained cocker spaniel might break loose and bark into the bog frightening off the residents in clucking droves before the army had fired a shot. Ill-tempered veterans were known to shoot such maverick hounds shrieking at their owners to 'take 'em home and teach 'em manners'.

But back to the chase: Hopes-Helis, living so far away, bought one of the first private horse boxes ever seen in the county, so he could drive himself and his daughters all the way from Mallow to the meet. They caused great glee on the first occasion when, arriving to the appreciative applause of the viewing public, he opened the doors of the newly acquired vehicle to discover that in his excitement he had forgotten to put the horses in the box.

Ballinagarde

In such circles of County Limerick the focus was on hunting; the levellers were horses. The Limerick Hunt didn't just begin with Toby Daresbury, it went back much further. In 1919 Colonel Henry Wyndham-Quin wrote *The Fox Hound in County Limerick* published by Maunsel in both Dublin and London.

> From the earliest ages the love of hunting, horses and hounds seems to have been inherent in the Irish race. It is one subject, perhaps the only one, upon which all classes and all creeds are in agreement, and its popularity has remained unimpaired throughout the many feuds and dissentions to which their country has been for so long subjected (1).

Henry describes how at some time in 1820 an undated invitation 'to form a Fox Hunting Club in the County of Limerick on a more extended scale,' was circulated. The movement was well supported (on the committee, among nine others were Joseph Gubbins of Kilfrush and John Croker of Croom Castle) but foremost was Edward Croker of Ballinagarde, who, in addition to a handsome subscription, presented his fine pack of fox hounds for the use of the hunt (34). Ballinagarde, now derelict, in Ballyneety, Co. Limerick, was built in 1774 by the Croker family who came originally from Devon in England.

One day towards the end of March 1830, the hounds met at Ballingarde. Mr Croker had been for some time indisposed, but his illness taking a turn for the worse, his second son, the Rev. Edward Croker, rector of Croom, was sent for to be with him. On coming downstairs the morning of the meet, the rector was somewhat astonished to find his father seated in a wheel chair in the hall, hunting-horn in hand and attired in the full costume of the chase. 'I am determined,' said he, 'both to see and hear the hounds once more, even though it be for the last time. Wheel me to the window.' Gazing on the (37) assembled pack, he then essayed to blow his horn, but strength failing him, he sent a message desiring the huntsman to sound the familiar notes for him. After listening for some moments to the horn, and the answering music of the hounds, Mr Croker turned his head from the window and raising his eyes, exclaimed, as it were to himself, 'Sweet Ballinagarde, must I leave you?' 'Father,' said the rector, 'fear not, for you may soon be going to an even brighter and better place than this.' 'I doubt it, Edward, I doubt it,' replied the old man mournfully . . . a few hours later he ceased to breathe (38).

Oliver St John Gogarty wrote a poem about Croker of Ballinagarde, which ended:

> He tried to persuade him and make him resigned,
> On Heavenly mansions to fasten his mind.
> "There's a Land that is Fairer than this," he declared.
> "I doubt it!" said Croker of Ballinagarde.[18]

'I doubt it, says Croker,' became a catchphrase in County Limerick; scattered through conversations ranging from marriage to the weather. 'I hear he's going to marry into one of the Limerick families?' 'I doubt it, says Croker.' 'Is the weather is going to improve at the weekend?' 'I doubt it, says Croker.'

Two years after taking on Tony Tarry as joint-master, Toby made it a triumvirate and the Earl of Harrington became joint master in 1972.

Bill Harrington was made of sterner stuff. A passionate huntsman, he rode out at least four days a week, keeping some fifty hunters for himself and his family at Greenmount Stud, Patrickswell, on the site of the present-day Limerick racecourse. He was joint master from 1972 to 1993 and

---

18   *The Poems and Plays of Oliver St John Gogarty*, edited by A. Norman Jeffares, London, Colin Smythe, 2001, p. 83.

again from 1997 until his retirement in 2001. His ancestor, the 1st Earl of Harrington, was Lord Lieutenant of Ireland from 1746 to 1751.

Born in 1922, Bill Harrington was only seventeen when the Second World War broke out. He would tell you himself that he had arrested Grand Admiral Karl Doenitz, President of the German Reich and Supreme Commander of the Armed Forces, in Flensburg at the end of that war. As Bill was only a Lieutenant at the time, Admiral Karl was insulted and asked to see his commanding officer. Bill was having none of it and neither would we. No one in Limerick would have him spoil a great story by demanding a more worthy capturing hero.

Raised at Elvaston Castle in Derbyshire, Bill succeeded to the Earldom at the age of seven when his father broke his neck in a hunting accident. His mother Margaret grew up at Mount Coote Stud in Kilmallock, Co. Limerick, where Bill spent a good deal of his childhood. In February 1942, the 19-year-old Earl married the first of his three wives, Eileen, only daughter and heiress of Sir John Foley-Grey of Enville Hall, Stourbridge. They had three children, Jane, Avna and his firstborn son, Charles, (known in Limerick as Viscount Petersham) now the 12th Earl of Harrington.

In 1946, Bill divorced his first wife and married Ann Chute, an heiress from Patrickswell, Co. Limerick. They had three children; Trina Maria and the twins, Steven Francis Lincoln and Sarah Sue. During the 1960s, Bill formed the Irish Olympic Horse Society and raised enough money to send Ireland's first ever three-day event team to the Olympic Games. As chairman of the Irish Thoroughbred Breeders' Association, he persuaded Charles Haughey, then Minister of Finance, to give tax breaks to horse breeders. Bill, alias William Henry Leicester Stanhope, 11th Earl of Harrington, passed away at his home The Glen, under Knockfierna, on Easter Sunday 2009 at the age of 86. He had bought the house and come to live there with his third wife Cilla in 1964, and Cilla still lives in the original Hederman house, The Glen, under Knockfierna.

III

The New Aristocracy

'A pump in the yard, a bull in the field, a son in the priesthood,' three signs you had made it. For big families, as most Catholic families were, priesthood and religious life were avenues towards betterment. Advancement to 'the altar' meant, for many, a distinct shift in social status: an otherwise unthinkable university education, a profession with guaranteed income, universal respect from the general public. Pressure applied from parents and teachers sought aggrandizement for potential candidates, but also reflected glory for themselves. Conversations could be overheard on buses: 'He's not great at the books, he'll never make it as a Jesuit; he's good at the football, we might send him to the Vincentians.'

Few men in Ireland in the thirties, forties and fifties of the twentieth century, did not see a path towards possible priesthood. Even without direct external pressure, the general atmosphere was such that few adolescents growing up at the time failed to think at some point or other of becoming a priest.

Until free second-level education was announced in an unauthorised speech by the Minister for Education, Donogh O'Malley on Saturday, 10th September,1966 educational opportunities for young people in Ireland were limited. Four out of every five children born between 1931 and 1941 were forced to emigrate. Primary education was free but secondary education was open to very few. Secondary schools were fee-paying and were mainly junior seminaries run by the Church to educate those they hoped would later become priests. The direct route from school to seminary was approved and applauded. Many young people struck by high-minded spiritual longing, combined with a craving for acceptance and acclaim, declared themselves ready. Once on the conveyor belt, it was difficult to get off; the stigma of being a 'spoilt priest' kept the timid and fainthearted in harness.

His father had longed to be a priest. Some years before ordination a break-down had him sent home. A lean-to out house was constructed against the wall of the home farm where he stayed in isolation until he 'got over his set-back'. A girl from the neighbouring farm was offered as collateral for merger with the farm next door. Their marriage produced eight children and doubled their acreage. The new paterfamilias became obsessed about having one of his sons ordained a priest. The prospects of all other family members were curtailed to allow the chosen boy to attend a local seminary. The question of vocation was irrelevant. He had the health, the funds and the Leaving Certificate; it was a question of doing what you were told and sticking it out. When authorities in the seminary told the father to take him home, that he had no vocation to the priesthood, his father took drastic action. He sent the young man to Australia where a distant relative was running a seminary. Here his son could continue his studies towards ordination. A year later, when it was established that the young man had neither interest in nor vocation to the priesthood, they sent him home for good. The father sent a younger member of the family to meet his brother dockside with the message that he was never to set foot inside the family home again. A spoilt priest was a disgrace to the family.

Priests who made it were hoisted to a platform where they were paraded as paragons of virtue. A scene from the film version of the musical *Grease* portrays a similar disconnect in Italian Catholic families: mother is serving lunch to her numerous noisy children. Behind them on the wall is a large framed picture of their elder brother, her son, dressed in priestly attire. He is in the local seminary awaiting ordination. As mother passes on her rounds of the table, she curtsies in reverence to the picture of her priestly son. The portrait is immaculate and aloof. Later, when this same son leaves the seminary and returns to his place at table with the rest of his siblings, his mother keeps the picture in place. At the same moment as she thumps the miscreant priest on the head for misbehaviour at table, she again curtsies to his picture on the wall behind. The idealised vision of her son the priest remains untainted.

Irish people had unrealistic, high-minded expectations of their clergy and no amount of evidence to the contrary could tarnish this image. Three men working on a pavement outside a brothel are shocked to see a Protestant minister and later a Jewish Rabbi pass them by and slink in through the doorway of the house of ill repute. 'Disgraceful' the men say to each other, 'these people, setting themselves up as examples for the rest of us.' They continue their work with self-satisfied contempt. A Catholic priest, well known to them all, approaches the doorway and enters. They nod in agreement: 'One of the girls must be sick.'

This new aristocracy was presented on display in 1932 at the Eucharistic Congress in Dublin. Between that event and the arrival of Pope John Paul II in 1979, half a century of adulation for priesthood unfolded. A completely unrealistic aura surrounded the idealised state for which so many young men were being prepared. Equivalent standards and expectations were demanded of them for the rest of their lives from an adoring population once they were ordained. Ordination changed the frog into a prince.

The 31st International Eucharistic Congress, held in Dublin in 1932, was certainly one of the most remarkable public events to have taken place in Ireland in the twentieth century. It generated a level of national enthusiasm that has few parallels.[19] With extremely favourable

19 Rory O'Dwyer, 'On Show to the World: The Eucharistic Congress, 1932, *History Ireland*, Vol. 15, Issue 6, Nov/Dec., 2007.

weather conditions in the run-up to and during the event, the country was in festive mood. The sheer scale of the conference bore striking testimony to the pride in identity, both national and religious, which guided the hundreds of thousands of people who participated. It took place over five days (22–26 June) in Dublin with a remarkable number of prestigious Irish ecclesiastics taking part. Waterford-born Archbishop of Sydney, Michael Kelly, Cardinal Patrick Hayes, Archbishop of New York, along with many of the dominant figures of the Catholic Church in the United States, who were either Irish-born or of immediate Irish descent, such as the Archbishop of Boston, William O'Connell, together with numerous other notable Irish-American prelates. Among the many non-Irish dignitaries were the Catholic primate of Poland, Cardinal Hlond, the Archbishop of Malines (Belgium), Cardinal Van Roey and the Archbishop of Paris, Cardinal Verdier.

The Men's Mass, held in the 'Fifteen Acres' of the Phoenix Park on 23rd June in front of a giant altar flanked by colonnades, was attended by a congregation of approximately 250,000. The Women's Mass on 24th June was attended by some 200,000 women. The Children's Mass on 25th June saw approximately 100,000 children gather in the Park. The main pontifical High Mass on 26th June was attended by an estimated million. This Mass featured a live broadcast by Pope Pius XI from the Vatican, transmitted via the most extensive PA system ever used before anywhere in the world, with loudspeakers located in the park, along the city quays and in various city centre locations. John McCormack sang the offertory motet, *Panis Angelicus*, to a captivated audience. G.K. Chesterton was one of the many journalists to hand.

The congress presents a snapshot of a period in Irish history when levels of religious devotion were at an apex. It also demonstrated that the Irish Free State was, to all intents and purposes, Catholic.

From then on the story could only have been one of decline. By the time Pope John Paul II made his historic visit to Ireland in 1979, far from being a triumphant show-case display of 2.7 million Catholics turning out to greet him, this super-star pageant was a last ditch stand for Roman Catholic Ireland. Already in 1979, after two decades of rapid economic growth, openness to the outside world and sweeping universal cultural changes, the Catholic Church in Ireland was openly in decline. The acknowledged purpose of the Irish hierarchy's invitation to Pope John Paul II was to halt or at least slow down damaging inroads to the ancient Catholic faith of Ireland.[20]

These two outstanding bookends enclose a period of forty years during which the new aristocracy were installed, took over, peaked and dissolved. The devastation from the wreckage would be cataclysmic. The Chapel at St Patrick's College Maynooth has 454 carved oak stalls for seminarians and priests. These run in serried ranks down the length of the nave, making it the largest choir chapel in the world. Founded in 1795 as the national seminary for the Catholic Church in Ireland, Maynooth has trained over 11,000 priests —not just for Ireland, but for the global church.

When construction began on the College Chapel in 1875, Maynooth was already the largest seminary in all of Christendom. Writing in *The Furrow* for January 1952, P.J. Brophy paints the picture: Today we have in Ireland eight colleges devoted to the formation of the secular clergy: Maynooth is the national seminary; Carlow, Clonliffe, Kilkenny, Thurles, Waterford and Wexford are diocesan seminaries, while All Hallows College trains priests exclusively for service outside Ireland. When Maynooth became a pontifical university and a recognised college of the National University of Ireland, it virtually relieved the diocesan seminaries of their primary function of training priests for service in Ireland. This meant that the other five colleges at Carlow, Kilkenny, Thurles, Waterford and Wexford formed priests for service abroad. 'No other country, Brophy continues, 'can boast of so many establishments of diocesan clergy serving the needs of dioceses scattered

----

20 Thomas Bartlett, *The Cambridge History of Ireland, Volume IV, 1880 to the Present*, Cambridge University Press, 2018, p. xxxi.

all over the world. ... keeping pace with and stimulated by British colonial expansion of the nineteenth century.' The acknowledgement of the forerunning British Empire is indicative; Ireland by mid-twentieth century had already established its own spiritual empire.

Ireland's spiritual empire

The idea of an 'Irish Empire' was a popular source of pride for politicians and priests, especially during the depressed periods after independence. 'There was a set of apparently cogent reasons for Catholics to believe that mass emigration from Ireland was part of a divine plan. History, a much-vaunted purity and strength of faith in the face of persecution, knowledge of an increasingly universal language, and the opening up to a great stream of Irish emigrants of empires political and mercantile, appeared to have converged in timely fashion to create a perfect missionary storm.'[21]

Michael O'Connor, Bishop Emeritus of Pittsburgh who later became a Jesuit, delivered a lecture in Philadelphia on St Patrick's Day 1864 'On the Destiny of the Irish Race'. This is one example, among many, of the heady mix of theology and history which 'proves' that the Irish were selected out of all other countries in the world to spread Catholicism (the only means of salvation) to the four corners of the earth. O'Connor, whose family came from Ireland, was a friend of Paul Cullen, having studied with him at the Urban College of the Propaganda in Rome. The lecture was, therefore, published in the *Irish Ecclesiastical Record*, the journal established by Cullen in 1864 as the official organ of Catholic thought in and from this country. The editorial for (November 1864) expatiates: 'In order to give to our readers the beautiful lecture of the ex-Bishop of Pittsburgh we have increased the number of pages in this month's RECORD.'

This lengthy piece, given here in summary, elaborates the theological argument which is simple enough: God created everything in the world

---

21   Sarah Roddy, 'Spiritual imperialism and the mission of the Irish race: the Catholic Church and emigration from nineteenth-century Ireland,' *Irish Historical Studies*, Vol. xxxviii no 152, November 2013, pp. 600-619.

and is in charge of everything that happens therein. England apostatised from the true religion and thereby gained the worldly prominence it now enjoys, having sold its soul to Satan. Its empire reaches to the ends of the earth. Ireland remained faithful to the true religion and can now follow in the wake of the empire builders (as Christianity did on the back of the Roman Empire), spreading the true seed of the Gospel on the newly harrowed soil. If the English had treated Ireland fairly the outcome might have been different: we might even have compromised, joined with them, lost our faith and become one of the greedy conquerors. But British persecution of the Irish saw to it that God's plan was brought to completion. The persecuted Irish kept their faith as the only thing left to them. Driven from their homes, deprived of their language and forced to learn English, they became ideal perpetrators of the heavenly plan. The providential famine forced them to emigrate. Now able to speak English they could bring to the countries where that language was becoming a universal tongue the benefits of the one true faith without which all these unfortunate people would be deprived of salvation.

This simple interpretation of some very stark and brutal facts of history convinced many Catholics at the time. To understand why, it is necessary to read some of the text itself to savour the rhetoric which made the specious argument so persuasive:

> That God knows and governs all things — that whatever happens is either done or permitted by him, and that he proposes to himself wise and beneficent ends in all he does or permits — are truths which lie at the foundation of all religion.
>
> It is in this view that many Christian writers assert that the Roman Empire obtained universal sway, that civilized nations being thus brought closely together, an easier way might be prepared for the spread of the Gospel. The generals and statesmen of Rome had no doubt a very low idea of the poor fishermen of Galilee, and of the tentmaker of Tharsus. It may be safely presumed that

they did not even allow their names to divert their thoughts, for a moment, from the grand projects of conquest and government by which they were engrossed. Yet, in the designs of God, it was, most probably, to prepare a way for the work of those fishermen, and of that tentmaker, and their associates, that wisdom had been vouchsafed to their counsels and victory to their arms.

The history of Ireland is, in many respects, peculiar. Few nations received the faith so readily, and no other preserved it amidst similar struggles ... We thus find God preparing Ireland for a future, then hidden to all but Himself.

In the sixteenth century England abandoned the faith to which she had adhered for a thousand years. Her apostasy, though consummated by degrees, may be said to have become at last complete.

The Irishman, generally speaking, did not leave home through ambition, or for conquest. He departed with sorrow from the shade of that hawthorn around which the dearest memories of childhood clustered. He would have remained content with the humble lot of his father had he been allowed to dwell there in peace. But the bailiff came, and, to make wider pastures for sheep and bullocks, his humble cottage was levelled, and he himself sent to wander through the world in search of a home. But in his wanderings he carries his faith with him, and he becomes the means of spreading everywhere the true Church of God.

It is thus that the tempest, which seems but to destroy the flower, catches up its seeds and scatters them far and near, and these seeds produce other flowers as beautiful as that from which they were torn, so that some fair spot of the prairie, when despoiled of its loveliness, but affords the means of covering the vast expanse with new and variegated beauties.

It is thus that the famine, and the pestilence, and the inhuman evictions of Irish landlords, have spread the faith of Christ far and near, and planted it in new colonies, which, when they shall have grown out of their tutelage, will look back to the departed power of England and the undying faith of Ireland as, in the hands of Providence, the combined causes of their greatness and their orthodoxy.

It is thus that the Catholic faith is being planted in the British colonies of North America; it is thus it is carried to India, and to Australia, and to the islands of the South Sea. Thus are laid the foundations of flourishing churches, which promise, at no distant day, to renew, and even to surpass, the work done by Ireland in the palmiest days of faith, when her sons planted the Cross, and caused Christ to be adored, as he wished to be adored, in the most distant regions of the earth.

Catholicity in the various other countries in which the English language is spoken.

The sufferings of Ireland were, therefore, the means, and evidently intended by God as the means to preserve her in the faith, to give her its rewards in a high degree; and this preservation of her faith was as evidently intended to make her and her sons instruments in spreading that faith throughout the English-speaking world. This is, therefore, what I claim to be, in the counsels of God, the destiny of the Irish Race.

Did we endeavour to draw this conclusion by far-fetched arguments, we might fear the delusions of fancy, but I think it is plainly written in the facts to which I have alluded, when looked at with faith in an overruling Providence. The diffusion of the true faith enters too closely, and is too primary a thing in the designs of God, to suppose it for a moment to be the work of accident. It is his work first of all. Where it exists it exists because he so willed it. The instruments that effected it must be those which he has chosen and placed to the work with this very view.

England may despise the Irish Catholic. Like Rome, she may look upon the professors of Catholicity as the great plague-spot of her system. Yet, in the designs of God, she most probably is indebted for her power to the part she is made to act in the diffusion of their faith. It is certain, at least, that the highest use of that power she has yet been allowed to make, is the carrying of frieze-coated Papists to distant shores, and the clearing of the forests where they are propagating, and are yet to propagate more extensively, the true faith.

The value and importance of this great mission cannot be overrated. It is awful to think what would have been the condition of the English-speaking races, in a religious point of view, if Ireland had shared in the English apostasy. Scarcely a Catholic voice would be heard amongst those seventy or eighty millions now using that language, who occupy so large a portion of the Earth, and in another century, according to the ratio of their growth, may become two or four hundred millions, or even more.

Is not this great result worth all the sufferings which Ireland has endured? The ways of God appear often circuitous. But in their circuitous course they are everywhere fraught with blessings. The children of Ireland suffered; yet, even in their sufferings they were blessed. He himself pronounced "blessed those who suffer persecution for justice's sake"; for in their trials they redeemed their own souls. But they were doubly blessed, because they were preserving the ark of God, and carrying it through the waters of tribulation to bless more amply unborn and numerous generations.

But, who knows what might have been the result, if justice and humanity had marked the course of the English nation towards Ireland? Who knows but the temptation to the latter to be drawn into apostasy would have been too powerful? Had Apostate England dealt generously or justly with Catholic Ireland, who knows if, in the alliances that would have been formed, she would have been equally steadfast in her faith? And though for a long time confiscations, and plunder, and persecution, and slaughter, and even now, harsh treatment condemning her sons to famine and banishment, have been the effects of the English connection; if these have been the means of creating a barrier that prevented the spread of heresy amongst her sons, has too great a price been paid for the "pearl" that has been bought? When, particularly, the cross borne by the children of Ireland shall have been erected in the Western and Southern [pg 087] Hemispheres, and flourishing Churches in Catholic unity established under its shade, where, but for the fidelity of our fathers, heterodoxy alone would have had sway, shall we not say that little indeed were their sufferings compared to the value of such an Apostolate of Empires?

Were we also to prove faithless to the mission which God has assigned us, we know not what punishment may await us, even in this world. The trials through which our race has passed, and is passing, may seem severe; but, they are trials permitted by a loving father. May we never deserve that he should scourge us in his great anger. We might then find, like the Jewish people, that to suffer for righteousness' sake from the hands of men, is sweet, compared to the gall and wormwood mixed in the cup of those who fall into the hands of an avenging God.

I would fain say to every son of Ireland — to everyone in whose veins Irish blood flows, no matter where he himself was born: Let us live worthy of our ancestry, of an ancestry which is the same for all, and is a noble one, noble in that which is the noblest thing man can rejoice in — virtue and fidelity to God.

Not even the most poignant and pathetic plea from such an authority as the Archbishop of Toronto in 1864 describing the plight of the recently emigrated Irish in terms of poverty, penury and hopelessness, where their supposed missionary mandate and activity extended only to bars and places of prostitution, could dissuade the bishops and leaders of the Catholic Church in Ireland from so distorted and wrongheaded a view of our history and our supposed destiny. Many huge ungainly buildings scattered around the country from the middle of the twentieth century, intended to house the army of candidates seduced by the grandeur of this project and prepared to offer their lives to its fulfilment, now stand empty and idle as monuments to its unreality.

Two chronologies

Two chronologies starting in the sixteenth century provide the warp and woof of this tapestry: the first is the calendar of events which led to the attempted suppression of Catholic worship in Ireland; the second is the establishment of the Tridentine Mass as the only form of Roman Catholic Eucharistic worship throughout the world. The Council of Trent was an Ecumenical Council of the Roman Catholic Church which was held between December 13, 1545 and December 4, 1563. The term 'Tridentine' came from the Latin word *Tridentinus*, from the city in which the Council was held, Tridentum (modern day Trent) in Italy.

If we remember the dates of Martin Luther, 1483-1546, it is easy to understand that the Council of Trent was as much as anything else a reaction to the threat of Protestantism. Much of the time of the council fathers was spent issuing anathemas against various Protestant heresies. This Council was an embodiment of 'the counter-reformation'.

In an attempt to centralise, regularise and standardise Roman Catholic worship, and in direct response to a decision of the Council of Trent, Pope Pius V promulgated the 1570 Roman Missal, making it mandatory throughout the Western Church, except in those regions and religious orders whose existing missals dated from before 1370. As well as being a riposte to the Reformation, the Council of Trent saw itself also as counteracting the worst abuses which had crept into the Roman Catholic Church during the first 1500 years of its existence; abuses which served as grist to the Protestant mill.

The *Missale Romanum ex decreto Sacrosancti Concilii Tridentini* (The Roman Missal issuing from the Council of Trent) 'began the period of iron uniformity in liturgy' which was to last until the Second Vatican

Council. Two principles of uniformity and immutability were to mark Catholic identity especially in worship, and this identity was to be safeguarded beyond all cultural difference. 'It was above all the Roman Congregation of Rites, which was founded in 1588 which took care of the Tridentine unified liturgy in its outward performance. Nothing was ever to be added, removed or altered.'[22] So, from 1570 to 1969, a period of 400 years, Roman Catholics anywhere around the world would recognise the same Liturgy of the Eucharist in Latin, no matter which church in the world they happened to enter at whatever time for those four hundred years.

This ritual was and is very splendid, very consoling, very mystical. It had and has enormous attraction for generations of practising Catholics. It is the ritual which every one of us who are over 70 would have been brought up with, if we were born into the Roman Catholic Church anywhere in the world.

However, being an Irish Catholic made this even more poignant. Let me outline the second time warp sketchily and hastily, which covers in parallel a similar time frame from the seventeenth century onwards: At the beginning of that century, James I came to the English and Irish thrones. In 1605 there was the Gunpowder Plot, a failed assassination attempt against King James by a group of English Catholics, whose plan was to blow up the House of Lords during the state opening of parliament on the 5th November, 1605. The notorious Guy Fawkes, one of twelve conspirators, was put in charge of the explosives stockpiled and hidden in an undercroft to the House of Lords. Henry Garnet, head of the Jesuit Order in England, was told of the plot in confession. Unwilling to break the seal of this sacrament to disclose the plot, he was convicted of treason and associated his whole order with the revolutionaries.

It is impossible to establish the truth of what actually happened. But, whatever the truth of the situation, it is perfectly understandable

....

22   Michael Kunzler, *The Church's Liturgy*, Continuum, London, 2001, p. 186.

that after the discovery of such a wide-ranging conspiracy, the capture of those involved, and the subsequent trials, Parliament would be led by the general panic and outrage to consider introducing new anti-Catholic legislation. Introducing an Oath of Allegiance to the king or queen seemed necessary under the circumstances, as was the stipulation requiring Catholics to abjure as a 'heresy' that 'princes excommunicated by the Pope could be deposed or assassinated'. In other words, it was no longer permitted for a Catholic, just because the Pope of the day refused to acknowledge the king or queen of your particular country, to ignore them, depose them, disobey their laws, and if the occasion presented itself, assassinate them in whatever way was most expeditious and least injurious to yourself. Any self-regarding monarch would have introduced similar restrictions against would-be assassins. The Popish Recusants Act of 1605 introduced a sacramental test, and an Oath of Allegiance.

An Irish rebellion took place in 1641. Cromwell undertook the definitive reconquest of Ireland from 1649 to 1653. Following the collapse of the Cromwellian regime in December 1659, Charles II was proclaimed King, the monarchy having been restored. He died in 1685. James II ascended the throne. When three years later he was removed, we have already seen how the Irish invited the ousted King, who was a Catholic, to lead them. Defeat at the Battle of the Boyne meant victory for the Protestant King William. However, just how much all this was a matter of politics rather than religion is signalled by the papal *Te Deum* which was sung in celebration of William's Boyne victory. It has also been revealed recently that Pope Innocent XI lent William of Orange 150,000 scudi through his family's bank, to help his progress, an embarrassing detail hidden from both Irish Catholics and Northern Protestants for over three centuries. The war ended in Ireland with the Treaty of Limerick in 1691 and 1695 marked the beginning of penal legislation enacted against Irish Catholics and Dissenters.

Such historical realities bolster the popular narrative about priesthood which captured the imagination of Irish people for several centuries. All of which required a conspiracy between a population hungry for hero-worship and a carefully cultivated storyline. The two potted histories of the background to such mythology are figments of the imagination as much as they are historical facts. They describe a psychological landscape fed into the minds of ordinary people. Whatever experience Catholics might have had of Mass during these difficult times would certainly have included furtive arrangements at secret places around the country. Mass might have happened in certain 'safe' houses or outside in the open air. Usually, the priest arrived in disguise and locals kept a look-out from vantage points for spies or soldiers.

The Irish countryside is littered with so-called Mass rocks still considered to be special sacred places. If you visit Glenstal Abbey in Limerick, for instance, you may be shown a leafy glade in the deep carved ravine of Cappercullen Glen, which was formed some one hundred million years ago. Sub-glacial phreatic flow is suggested as the architect by expert examination of existing evidence on the floor of the glen. Two house-sized blocks resting one on the other have been identified as 'a Mass Rock'. If you had come this way in the 1970s or 1980s, you might have stumbled across the Archbishop of Cashel and Emly concelebrating with the Abbot of Glenstal, an annual Mass of commemoration at this venue. The official 'historical guide' would inform you that 'the mass-rock was in use between 1650 and 1700'. Proof of this was the finding of a William III penny coin on the ground in the nearby vicinity. 'The people attending Mass in the glen could stand on either side of the deep ravine,' the guide continues, 'and there was the added advantage that someone could keep a good lookout for soldiers at the top of the glen.'

You might then be shown an early thirteenth century stone, and on the South-East wall of the chapel built around the rocks, an ancient carved Calvary with Christ on the cross flanked by Mary and John, defaced, you again might be told, by seventeenth century puritans. All of which is well-meaning make-believe. 'It is easy to see', says David Fleming, 'how unreliable oral testimony can metamorphose into even more dubious folklore.' In *The Soul of Ireland* (1920) W.J. Lockington SJ gives a whole chapter to the Mass Rock depicted as the Calvary of Ireland, with the priest represented as the sacrificed Christ:

> Gaze at that dark stain on the gray stone. Oh, how it speaks to us of the lonely mountain in the silent dawn, the shadowy forms gathering and crouching on the grass, the priest holding God aloft, the loud cry of alarm sounding through the gloom from the posted sentries; the low moan of misery from the broken-hearted kneelers, the flash of the musket, the priest lying across the stone, dyeing it with his life-blood – still clasping the chalice to his breast – dead.[23]

There was a conflation of two distinct periods of history and two separate punitive campaigns. The Cromwellian War in Ireland began in 1649 and lasted for five years. Cromwell himself was in Ireland for nine months only. His aim was suppression of rebellion and complete conquest of the Confederate and Royalist coalition which had coalesced in Ireland. His invasion was military and political. This was a particular period of brutal suppression of Jacobite insurgency in Ireland. Cromwell's whole project collapsed in 1659 in both England and Ireland when kingship was reinstated and Charles II began his reign. This period, therefore, concerned a ten-year period in the seventeenth century.

The Penal Laws, on the other hand, which dominated most of the eighteenth century, were passed by the Protestant Parliament of Ireland itself in an attempt to regulate the status of Roman Catholics in this country. The declared purpose was to disenfranchise the native majority from political and economic power. The laws were aimed not at a particular race or ethnic group, but at the adherents of a particular religion. The ideal was to entice the colonised Irish into wholesale conversion to

---

23   W.J. Lockington, *The Soul of Ireland*, London, 1919, p. 51.

Protestantism. A Catholic could avoid the oppressive effects of these laws by conversion, although the statutes went to great lengths to ferret out insincere conversions.

Cardinal Patrick Francis Moran, as far away as Sydney, published his account of *The Catholics of Ireland under the penal laws* in 1899. He provides a near-living example of a Mass-rock witness in the person of the recently deceased Bishop of Raphoe, Patrick McGettigan (1815-87), who in his childhood 'was often placed on the summit of a high rock to signal the approach of priest hunters, whilst in the adjoining hollow the assembled parishioners huddled to hear Mass'. But, as Fleming points out, there were no 'priest hunters' in Ireland in the first half of the nineteenth century and no reason whatsoever for McGettigan to be standing guard.

In the early 1970s some of the monks at Glenstal Abbey constructed this crude chapel using poured concrete over sitka spruce poles, steel frame beds and bicycles, into which they inserted carved stones from the nearby medieval abbey of Abington. There is no proof that such a venue was ever used for the celebration of Mass at any time before the twentieth century. The only people ever historically recorded as having said Mass in this romantic glade are the Archbishop of Cashel and Emly and the Abbot of Glenstal in the final decades of the twentieth century. And the only persecution endured was from midges which ate them alive in the summer months of those two decades.

The point being made is that such fabricated evidence and wishful myth-making has been impressed upon a whole landscape around Ireland, supposedly dotted with Mass rocks. Recent scholarship has shown that most of these sites result from nineteenth or twentieth century reconstruction rather than any factual basis in history. 'Many of the popular notions of the "Mass rock" derive from the formal curriculum of primary schools from the nineteenth century onwards ... The Catholic Church itself was the main promoter of the "Mass rock" in the twentieth century ... encouraging pilgrimages to such sites.'[24] All of which was part of a studied attempt to establish the Mass and the priest in Catholic imagination as fixed stars in a projected cosmology.

The alternative venue for Mass was in people's homes. Word was put about locally that Mass would be said in a particular house on a particular day. The neighbours would gather for what was often the only opportunity to be at Mass for a long time. Because it was not safe for the priest to carry sacred vessels or vestments with him on his journeys, these were taken care of by the local people. They passed the 'Mass kit' from house to house as it was needed. Catholic clergy were expelled from the country and were liable to instant execution if found in Ireland. Four hundred priests had been deported by 1698 and the country was without a Catholic archbishop from 1692 to 1714. Such memories are kept alive in local areas. Seventeen Catholic martyrs from this period were beatified in 1992. So, two things about these priests who visited their flocks to say Mass in danger of their lives: they appeared like Robin Hood out of nowhere and were venerated as heroes and became sainted martyrs in the eyes of the faithful. This adulatory aura around priests lasted until the last quarter of the twentieth century.

And many of these objects of veneration were trained to be priests in seminaries or universities abroad. Here they would have been steeped in the liturgy and rubrics which had been laid down in 1570. The essential thrust of such training in all its minutely prescribed detail is that the Mass remains always the priest's work, and its purest form is present in the private Mass which could be said by any priest on his own with only one Mass server representing the people of God.[25]

The Tridentine Mass took on the aura of a sacred and untouchable rite. It became almost a magic formula to the point of superstition.

....

24 David A. Fleming, 'The "Mass rock" in eighteenth-century Ireland: the symbolic and historical past,' in *Church and Settlement in Ireland*, eds. James Lyttleton & Matthew Stout, Dublin: Four Courts Press, 2018, pp. 182-207.

25 Michael Kunzler, *The Church's Liturgy*, Continuum, London, 2001, p. 191.

The actual moment where the bread and wine were changed into the body and blood of Christ became identified with the consecration. *Hoc est enim corpus meum* (from which emerges the disparaging expression 'Hocus Pocus' meaning nonsense formulae uttered by cunning tricksters or rogue magicians). These words of consecration over the host and the chalice, became the focal point for the actual deed done during Mass.[26] People spoke of 'getting Mass' if they were there for the consecration. A parish priest in Cabinteely in the 1970s measured the time between the last person arriving at his church and the first person leaving, on an average Sunday morning. Seven and a half minutes was his reckoning.

Priests developed scrupulous fixations about saying the words of consecration correctly. Some would take a long time to stammer their way through the sacred formulae: *HHHHoc es-es-est enim* etc. Altar boys at private Masses would dread being landed with one of the obsessives and would regale their fellow servers with hilarious imitations of their stammering prelate. Films were made and stories told about priests who uttered the magic words of consecration in brothels and restaurants; or about people who absconded with the magic particles to use their power in different circumstances for good or ill.

Le Défroqué (1954) a French film directed by Léo Joannon caused shock waves throughout a culture imbued with Catholic sensibility. The climax of irreverence depicted an ex-priest who, to scandalise a young man thinking of being ordained, says the words of Consecration over a glass of wine in a restaurant. The film wasn't actually banned in Ireland but the climactic scene of desecration was excised rendering the whole story line meaningless; Hamlet without the prince.

26 'The priest bent down to put it into her mouth, murmuring all the time. Latin. The next one. Shut your eyes and open your mouth. What? Corpus. Body. Corpse. Good idea the Latin. Stupefies them first. Hospice for the dying. They don't seem to chew it; only swallow it down. Rum idea: eating bits of a corpse. Why the cannibals cotton to it . . . Something like those mazzoth: it's that sort of bread: unleavened showbread. Look at them. Now I bet it makes them feel happy. Lollipop. It does. Yes, bread of angels it's called. There's a big idea behind it, kind of kingdom of God is within you feel. Fists communicants. Hokypoky penny a lump.' *Ulysses*, Episode 5: Lotus Eaters.

All of which points to a culture where the Eucharist had become a magical formula and the priest its singular magician. More importantly, it presents the whole salvific mystery of Jesus Christ on Calvary as something delivered wholly and entirely into the hands of priests.

In 1925 John Mary Vianney, the Curé d'Ars (1786-1859) was canonised by Pope Pius XI and in 1929 he was made patron saint of parish priests. One of his sermons on priesthood is pertinent: 'Without the priest, the death and passion of our Lord would be no use; the priest has the keys of the heavenly treasures... What is the priest? A man who holds the place of God, a man clothed with all the powers of God.'

A popular poem by an unknown author, used very often on ordination cards for priests, carries a similar message: the priest is the unique channel of salvation for the body of the faithful; their fate is in his hands:

The Beautiful Hands of a Priest

We need them in life's early morning,
we need them again at its close;
We feel their warm clasp of friendship,
we seek them when tasting life's woes.
At the altar each day we behold them,
and the hands of a king on his throne
Are not equal to them in their
greatness; their dignity stands all alone;
And when we are tempted and wander
to pathways of shame and sin,
It's the hand of a priest that will absolve
us - not once, but again and again;
And when we are taking life's partner,
other hands may prepare us a feast,
But the hand that will bless and unite
us is the beautiful hand of a priest.

God bless them and keep them all holy
For the Host which their fingers caress;
When can a poor sinner do better than
to ask Him to guide thee and bless?
When the hour of death comes upon us
may our courage and strength be increased.
By seeing raised over us in anointing the
beautiful hands of a priest!

Such total reliance on priestly hands bred two kinds of pathology, one in the priest, the other in the people. The priest is overwhelmed by the multitudes seeking the salvation which only these hands can produce. He himself becomes obsessed by his responsibility to provide such salvation during every moment of his waking life.

The Edge of Sadness is a novel written in 1961 by Edwin O'Connor. It was one of the ten bestsellers of the year, sharing the list with *The Agony and the Ecstasy, Franny and Zooey,* and *To Kill a Mockingbird.* It won the Pulitzer Prize for Fiction in 1962. Fr Hugh Kennedy, a middle-aged Catholic priest, is a recovering alcoholic returned to his home town to try to recover and mend his professional career as a priest.

He finds the situation intolerable. The people of the parish have become obsessively dependent on the ministrations of their priest. They expect him to be an ever-open ear to their every whine and moan. Far from understanding his vulnerability and need for recuperation, they see him as an indestructible shoulder to weep upon, an everlasting supply of Kleenex. 'They won't quit. Every day I get up, I walk across to the church, I say Mass – and that's the end of the day for me. Because then they begin to come in. Good God in heaven, how can people talk so much? It's endless.'[27]

He finds that the priest has become the universal ear for people deprived of basic social and human contact. Not that they expect any

27 Edwin O'Connor, *The Edge of Sadness*, Loyola Classics Paperback, 2005.

guidance or advice from the whipping boy. His job is to shut up and listen. Whenever he might intervene to offer a solution or stem the flow, he becomes a nuisance, an unwarranted pause in their endless tale of woe. Like the doctor in Axel Münthe's *Story of San Michaele*, to tell the patient there is nothing wrong with them, or to provide a definitive cure, is to prove your incompetence as a doctor, your disqualification from from your profession. 'My day is spent in listening to one continuous supplicating whine. There's always one thing more. Every day. The same old whimpers and whispers and groans and tears from people who can't manage their own lives and who can't wait to bolt down their breakfast before rushing up to the rectory to tell me they can't. And it's all nonsense; it means nothing. I'm a priest, not a wastepaper basket.'

Fr Robert Nash in his biography of Fr James Duff, former Professor of Classics at Maynooth, describes the priestly pathology:

> It is hardly an exaggeration to say that, from the day of his appointment, Castlewellan and its interests and its people became for him a sort of obsession. He was never wholly at ease when he was away from them. On his occasional visits to his sister in Dublin, he would explain that he must hurry home, as 'they' would be wanting him in the confessional or in his house. The people had the impression that they owned him, could turn to him at any time, seeking his advice or consolation or material help. He never would leave the church as long as there was a chance of somebody coming in for confession. Whatever he had was theirs. He listened to all worries but he never spoke of his own. He was there for only one purpose: to be at the disposal of any who wanted him for any reason at any time.

If over a year of lockdowns from Covid-19 has taught us anything, it might be that God does not need anyone's hands or anyone's ministry to reach out and touch each one of God's people. The sacred hands of the priest are just as likely to be a purveyor of disease as anyone else's. '*Noli me tangere*' – hands off everybody. Let God become present in whatever way God chooses to reveal Godself to whomsoever.

Hollywood aristocrats

A similar compulsion established an aristocracy of stardom in Hollywood during an equivalent twentieth century time span. Even now, as we advance through the twenty-first century, there is a certain undeniable elegance about old Hollywood movies. We like to think that it was a better, a more honourable time, when men were gentlemen and women were ladies. Chivalry still existed at that time, we sob to ourselves or to a Kleenex, and so did romance.

This was a deliberately cultivated mirage which huge money and effort maintained for half a century. At all costs preserve the image on the silver screen; ignore the mayhem in reality behind it. People need a Pantheon, and promoters of this projection were prepared to provide one whatever the price. 'Old Hollywood' cultivated the innocent and virginal image of their stars and a worldwide fan club was not just happy to believe but determined to keep it that way. Golden Age Tinsel Town spelt class, sophistication and stainlessness. Matinee idols chastely stole kisses in black and white. This was life as it should be. A later generation wised up, but at the time nobody thought that behind the glamour and the glitz, the real lives of the idols told a different story.

Clark Gable was more a Hollywood creation than a consummate actor. Coached by MGM executives from being an amateur stage presence to become the biggest movie star ever known, he managed to remain consistent box-office bounty. Why? Because people loved him. Why? Because he was tutored to imitate what the audience was taught to adore as 'the ideal man'. He was Rhett Butler in person. He swept beautiful women off their feet. Judy Garland sang for so many in 'Dear Mr Gable, You Made Me Love You':

Through every single window, I see your face
But when I reach the window there's only empty space.

His image, even 50 years after his death, is still the handsome, romantic, roguish charmer, even though his acting ability was threadbare and his private life, behind the scenes and along the way, unwholesome. Married five times, he was never faithful to any of his five wives. He had such a relentless fling with Joan Crawford that MGM threatened to fire them both for contravening the morality clauses in their contracts.

In the eyes of the public Clark was king and Hollywood's aristocracy accepted his coronation. They had no choice. He was the perfect fit for the kingly archetype. What matter if in his private life he was a serial seducer who ruthlessly plied his charms, particularly on older women in powerful positions on Broadway or Hollywood, to make his way to the top. Who cares if he was the proverbial 'toy boy' before the word had been invented. What we don't know doesn't trouble us, say the general public; and they didn't know and didn't want to know. His death marked the end of Hollywood's Golden Age. When 'the King' died, kingship died with him.

The public was exceedingly and cruelly demanding of their idols. If they did find out that the reality was not consistent with the image, their anger and vindictiveness were unrelenting. Behind Tinsel Town's glitzy facade loomed the spectre of Hollywood's 'sexual gestapo'. Vigilantes were too often eager to unmask the idols they begrudged, all too ready to feed high-priced scandal to gossip-greedy paparazzi. A host of matinee idols who were gay, for instance, led extravagantly contorted lives in the spotlight to keep the secret of their sexuality in the closet. All that mattered was to feed the public with the image they expected and accepted.

The fallout over Ingrid Bergman's personal life was a cautionary tale which leaves no doubt about the public's reaction to fallen idols. Married to Peter Lindstrom, she took up with the Italian director Roberto Rossellini while he was directing her in the film *Stromboli* in 1950. She became pregnant and they had a child. The pregnancy caused a huge scandal. Uproar from the general public, fanned by media supply of scorching hot copy, caused Bergman to be declared *persona non grata* on the floor of the United States Senate. A senator from Colorado described her as 'a horrible example of womanhood and a powerful influence for evil'. Forced into exile, she went to Italy, leaving her husband and daughter in the United States. Bergman and Rossellini began divorce proceedings against their respective spouses and got married in 1950. Rossellini was described by the media as a 'Nazi collaborator inspired by cocaine'. The government in the United States tried to introduce legislation which would make filmmakers and stars responsible for their behaviour, ordering them to apply for government permits in order to make films. These permits could be revoked at any time if anything morally ambiguous in their lives was detected.

Multiply all this by thousands when aristocracy hits royalty, when the star becomes nothing less than a princess, and she of Irish descent. Grace Kelly (1929–1982) after starring in several significant movies in the early to mid-1950s, became Princess of Monaco, marrying Crown Prince Rainier III in April 1956.

Grace had embarked on her acting career at the age of twenty, despite her wealthy father's disapproval (Jack Kelly saw actors as next door to 'street-walkers,' one step up from prostitution). Grace starred in several critically acclaimed and commercially successful movies, usually opposite male leads twenty-five to thirty years older than herself. John Ford's *Mogambo*, which also starred Ava Gardner and Clark Gable, brought her to the public eye. She made three Alfred Hitchcock suspense thrillers in rapid succession in 1954-55: *Dial M for Murder* with Ray Milland; *Rear Window* with James Stewart; and *To Catch a Thief* with Cary Grant. She retired from acting at the age of 26 to marry Prince Rainier, and took up her role as Princess of Monaco. Again her plainspoken Irish father disapproved: 'No daughter of mine is going to marry any damn broken-down prince who is head of a country over there that nobody ever knew anything about.' Hitchcock had hoped she would appear in more of his films, describing her as 'sex on ice'. He was unable to coax her out of retirement.

In 1956, just before her wedding, Grace Kelly starred with Alec Guinness in a film called *The Swan*. It was the movie of the preview. Princess Alexandra, played by Grace, is the daughter of a minor branch of a European royal house. She is urged by her mother to accept her cousin, crown prince Albert, played by Alec Guinness, so their family can regain a throne taken from them by Napoleon. The film was released the day before Grace became the Princess Consort of Monaco.

In the last Hitchcock film she made, *To Catch A Thief*, Monaco was the venue. In one startling scene Grace, playing Frances Stevens, drives much too fast across precarious Riviera mountain roads to help Cary Grant elude pursuing police. How strange in view of what happened later: that she would die driving along those same roads. Her life on screen ran parallel to the fairy story of her actual history. Or, was it the other way round?

And, of course, Princess Grace and Prince Rainier made a state visit to Ireland, to the home of her ancestors, in 1961. Her grandfather, John Peter Kelly, born in 1857, was a bricklayer from Newport in Mayo. He left Ireland in 1887 for Philadelphia where he founded a leading construction company and made his family's fortune. Grace visited Ireland on three occasions in 1961, 1976 and 1979. During her first trip, she went to the old cottage where her grandfather had lived, and she bought it along with 35 acres of land after her second visit in 1976.

Hers was the perfect story of a poor labourer from Ireland making it to the top in America. As far as the Irish were concerned nothing would ever tarnish this image. She was the archetype of physical beauty and unquestioned purity. Grace was Ireland's perfect princess. Several families of Kellys in Ireland were devastated that their invitation to the wedding in Monaco got lost in the post.

In five short years — 1951 to 1956 — the coolly beautiful actress wooed Hollywood audiences, not to mention a number of its leading men. After her untimely death at the age of 52, the gap between the reality and the mirage began to widen. Though she had made only 11 films in her brief acting career, she began to be linked to some of her older co-stars. While some — like Clark Gable (*Mogambo*) or Bing Crosby (*High Society*, *The Country Girl*) — were single at the time, others including Gary Cooper (*High Noon*), William Holden (also *The Country Girl*) and Ray Milland (*Dial M for Murder*) were married. Bing Crosby, who was her co-star in *High Society* and *The Country Girl* (the film which won her an Oscar) proposed to Grace when his wife died. Grace's mother approved the match because Crosby was a Catholic and a widower. Nothing came of it.

What would the Irish fans have made of the claim by film producer Robert Evans in his 2013 memoir, that the fairytale union between Grace and Prince Rainier was a business transaction brokered by Aristotle Onassis. He, who owned property in Monaco, sought to turn the postage-stamp-picturesque principality into a gambling mecca for the rich and famous. A glamorous Hollywood match was all that was required. 'The right bride could do for Monaco's tourism what the coronation of Queen Elizabeth did for Great Britain,' Rainier was told by Onassis, who was part of a syndicate of casino owners in Monaco.

We desperately need our idols. If they are smashed, we either refuse to believe the undeniable evidence before us and continue to worship, or we transfer our needy allegiance to a worthier simulacrum.

Two years after our Princess called, the Prince of all Princes arrived. The visit of John F. Kennedy to Ireland placed a masculine counterpart on the other side of the mantel-piece: Ireland's model of manhood had come home. The visit lived up to everyone's expectations. Kennedy referred to it as 'the best four days of my life'. It took place five months before his assassination.

As first US president to pay an official state visit to the Republic of Ireland, he was also the first Catholic president of that country and he was of pure bred Irish descent. Both his maternal and paternal families came from Ireland. And here's where Limerick comes into its own. The Fitzgerald family came from Bruff in Co. Limerick. Between 1846 and

1855, some of the Fitzgeralds migrated to America to escape the famine. On September 18, 1889 John Francis 'Honey Fitz' Fitzgerald married Mary Josephine Hannon of Acton, Massachusetts. She was the daughter of Michael Hannon and Mary Ann Fitzgerald, both born in Ireland. Their daughter, Rose Elizabeth Fitzgerald - born in Boston on July 22, 1890 - was John Fitzgerald Kennedy's mother.

At the same time that the Fitzgeralds migrated, Patrick Kennedy - a cooper from Dunganstown, Co. Wexford - sailed for the United States. In 1849, he married Bridget Murphy, born about 1827 in Owenduff, Co. Wexford. Nine years later she was a widow with four small children, the youngest of whom, Patrick Joseph Kennedy, would become John F. Kennedy's grandfather.

These undeniable irreproachable Irish-American genealogies made JFK number one in the litany of success stories we longed to hear. He became one of the striking talismans of twentieth-century Ireland imagery. Pictures of the Sacred Heart on which are emblazoned Jesus Christ and John F. Kennedy saturated the repository market. Two years after his visit to Ireland, the Cathedral of Our Lady Assumed into Heaven and St Nicholas in Galway was dedicated. In the baptistery there visitors still can see, if they remove the clutter deliberately arranged to try and hide it, a mosaic of the Crucifixion flanked by Padraig Pearse and JFK. These two, at the time of the triumphal opening of Galway cathedral, had become patron saints of twentieth century Ireland's need for home-grown archetypes of perfection.

It was only later that biographers began to debunk the theory that JFK's presidency was a reincarnation of Camelot, and his own lifestyle a mirror of saintliness. The carefully cultivated imagery of JFK as paragon of virtue, married to the most beautiful woman in the world; the family man upholding the basic unit of society and committed to his marriage vows, began to fade. It became clear that John F. Kennedy was possibly the most prolific philanderer ever to grace the Oval Office. The 35th President of the United States told the British Prime Minister, Harold Macmillan: 'If I don't have a lay every three days, I get a headache.'

It emerged also that not long after their glamorous wedding, Jackie was planning to divorce her husband but that her father-in-law had given her a million dollars to change her mind lest it damage his son's political ambitions. The ambition was more the father's than the son's. There is no doubt that Joe Kennedy Senior went to great lengths to push his children to heights he himself wished to reach. He had once entertained notions of running for the presidency. In 1940, before Franklin Roosevelt announced his candidacy for a third term, Kennedy, then the ambassador to Great Britain, was often mentioned in the papers as one of the half-dozen men likely to win the Democratic nomination. Yet if he was vain, he was also streetwise; he knew there was no way America at the time was ready to elect a Catholic as president. That would have to wait for another generation. His first choice was his eldest son Joe Junior. When Joe was killed in action in World War II in 1944, his father was devastated, but he lost no time in finding a substitute. John, as second son, assumed the mantle of his father's determined ambition. When JFK was later asked about the level of involvement and influence that his father had in his razor-thin presidential victory over Richard Nixon, he would joke that on the eve of the election his father had asked him the exact number of votes he would need to win: There was no way he was paying 'for a landslide'.

Such are the hazards of cultivated images. And yet, the cultivated image often outlasts the established facts. JFK, a moderately successful President of the United States remains an icon of twentieth century leadership. And we learn to our cost that mosaics, like tattoos, are difficult to remove when you begin to regret having put them on your baptistry.

The mechanisms in all such myth-making are the same: aggrandisement of the model; airbrushing of any perceived imperfection. There is always a gap between the idealised superstars and the flesh and blood reality. In the case of priests, they were presumed to be transposed by ordination to a miraculous sphere where all normal human energies were made holy and inoffensive. Disillusioned fury is unleashed when this garden of images is despoiled, not just by one or two erring exceptions but by a whole crumbling edifice of too many miscreants. Humpty Dumpty had indeed a great fall.

The devil's advocate

World-wide English-speaking literature in the twentieth century was saturated with stories about priests. Graham Greene (1904 – 1991) shortlisted for the Nobel Prize in 1966 and 1967, explored in his 25 novels the moral and political issues of his world, mostly from a Catholic perspective. One of his best known novels, *The Power and the Glory* (1940) won the Hawthornden Prize in England at the time of its publication and, in 2005, was chosen by *Time Magazine* as one of the hundred best English-language novels since 1923.

The main character is an unnamed 'whiskey priest',' working in Mexico, who has fathered a child in his parish some years previously. *The Power and the Glory* was seen as tarnishing the image of the missionary priest. Greene recorded that in 1953 the Archbishop of Westminster, Cardinal Bernard Griffin, read him a letter from the Holy Office condemning the novel because it was "paradoxical" and "dealt with extraordinary circumstances".

Meanwhile in Australia, Morris West (1916–1999), who had entered a Christian Brothers Seminary in Sydney at the age of 14 'as a kind of refuge from a difficult childhood,' became a writer whose novels were published in 27 languages and sold more than 60 million copies worldwide. West used Catholicism as the texture of his stories and the figure of the priest as a central character. One of his best known, *The Devil's Advocate* (1959), describes Fr Blaise Meredith, a dying English priest, who is sent from the Vatican to a small village in Calabria to investigate the life of Giacomo Nerone, a local hero being proposed for canonisation. Meredith discovers that Nerone was in fact a deserter from the British army, who had an illegitimate son by a local woman, and was executed by Communist partisans towards the end of World War II. *The Devil's Advocate* reveals the real life of the real man as in no way conforming to the airbrushed public image of the wannabe saint.

In *The Shoes of the Fisherman* (1963) he describes the election and career of a Slavic Pope, 15 years before the historic papacy of Karol Wojtyła as John Paul II. These books are hardly read anywhere nowadays, they were of their time and formed part and parcel of the world's obsession with priesthood.

Literature in Ireland was similarly saturated. Many Irish writers began their lives in a seminary. Brian Moore (1921–1999) was born in Belfast with eight siblings. His father was a convert to Catholicism and Brian himself went to St Malachy's College, the oldest Catholic Diocesan College on the island of Ireland. The college was founded four years after Catholic Emancipation in 1833. As well as one cardinal and six bishops, many former students went on to positions of influence. Brian Moore on the other hand left the college in 1939, having failed his final exams. The school at the heart of his novel *The Feast of Lupercal* (1957) is a fictionalised setting of the college as he remembered it.

His novel *Catholics* (1972) takes place on an island monastery off the southwest coast of Ireland some time near the end of the twentieth century after the Second Vatican Council. A young priest is sent by the authorities in Rome to call to order an Irish monastery that still celebrates the Catholic liturgy according to the older rite. The abbot of the monastery is agnostic and plagued by doubts in matters of faith. He accepts the newly imposed regime but sees it simply as a new liberal tyranny replacing an older conservative one. Both regimes are substitutes for any real connection with God.

Brian Friel (1929–2015), began his life on the road to priesthood. He left Maynooth after two years in the 1940s, where 'he explored the vocation which he believed he had to the priesthood'. He later said in 1972, when he was 43 years of age: 'I hope that between now and my death I will have acquired a religion, a philosophy, a sense of life, that will make the end less frightening than it appears to me at this moment.'[28]

Friel is the kind of playwright Yeats was promoting: 'I would like

---

28   Richard Pine, *Brian Friel and Ireland's Drama*, London, 1990, pp. 17-18.

to write a play that would capture the peculiar spiritual, and indeed material, flux that this country [Ireland] is in at the moment. This has got to be done, for me anyway . . . at local level, and hopefully this will have meaning for people in other countries. The canvas can be as small as you wish, but the more accurately you write and the more truthful you are, the more validity your play will have for the world.'[29]

Dancing at Lughnasa (1990) tells of a missionary priest sent home from Uganda because he has 'gone bush' or has been 'touched by the sun'. Instead of converting the 'pagans' to the religion he was sent out to preach, he was gradually being converted to their way of life, to their religion. Friel is prompting the scene silently from behind like a ritual or a spell. The play is a retrieval of something 'traditional', something Celtic. The festival of Lughnasa is a fertility rite to begin the harvest. As late as 1962, Maire MacNeill found 'Lughnasa being celebrated in Ireland on ninety-five heights and by ten lakes and five river banks'.[30] This play touched some deep chord in audiences everywhere, playing to packed houses in Dublin, New York and London, eventually being made into a major Hollywood film. It ends with Michael, the narrator of the story:

> When I remember it, I think of it as dancing. Dancing with eyes half closed because to open them would break the spell. Dancing as if language had surrendered to movement - as if this ritual, this wordless ceremony, was now the way to speak, to whisper private and sacred things, to be in touch with some otherness. Dancing as if the very heart of life and all its hopes might be found in those assuaging notes and those hushed rhythms and in those silent and hypnotic movements. Dancing as if language no longer existed because words were no longer necessary...[31]

....

29 *The Irish Times*, 12th February, 1970.
30 Maire MacNeill, *The Festival of Lughnasa*, Comhairle Bhealoideas Eireann, UCD, 1982.
31 Brian Friel, *Dancing at Lughnasa*, Faber, 1990, p. 71.

Friel talked, too, of the theatre as a 'theoretical priesthood'. In his plays the figures who most closely represent the artist are priests or priest-like: St Columba in The Enemy Within, Archbishop Lombard in Making History, Fr Jack in Dancing at Lughnasa and, above all Frank Hardy in Faith Healer.

For what is Frank's calling if not a kind of secular priesthood, or, as he calls it himself, 'a ministry without responsibility, a vocation without a ministry?' And what is the life of a writer if it is not also a vocation without a ministry? In declining his call to the priesthood, Friel found his vocation.[32]

For Seamus Heaney (1939–2013) the relationship between priest and poet is palpable, and in many poems such as 'The Forge' and 'The Tollund Man,' the poet takes on the role of a priest.

> I think Catholicism meant everything to me in some ways; because it was my whole life. I was at a Catholic boarding school, and the community I lived in moved on the poles of the Church and the Gaelic football team ... There was a sense of common culture about the place [his school, St Columb's College, Derry, Northern Ireland] we were largely Catholic farmers' sons being taught by farmers' sons. The idea of a religious vocation was in the air all the time; not a coercion by any means, but you would have to be stupid or insensitive not to feel the invitation to ponder the priesthood as a destiny.[33]

Heaney pursued such an invitation through his 'vocation' to poetry. 'Put simply, for Heaney ... the priestly role must be displaced from its doctrinal moorings. Yet the sheer necessity of the displacement shapes his counter vocation. As such, the role of priest is inevitably woven into his destiny as a poet.'[34] In his essay 'From Monaghan to the Grand Canal,' Heaney describes Paddy Kavanagh in words that might also describe

32   Fintan O'Toole, 'The Truth according to Brian Friel,' The Irish Times, 2nd October, 2015.
33   Neil Corcoran, The Poetry of Seamus Heaney, London, Faber and Faber, 1986, p. 116.
34   Daniel Tobin, Passage to the Center, University Press of Kentucky, 1999, p. 183.

himself in this role: 'a priest who has ordained himself and stands up in Monaghan, the celebrant of his own mysteries.'[35]

John McGahern (1934–2006) could be regarded as the Kafka and Proust of 1950s Ireland. His meticulous prose preserves for us tangible connection with what he referred to as 'the weather of those times'.

> Corpus Christi was summer. Rhododendron and lilac branches were taken by cart and small tractors from the Oakport Woods and used to decorate the grass margins of the triangular field around the village. Coloured streamers and banners were strung across the road from poles. Altars with flowers and a cross on white linen were erected at Gilligan's, the post office and at Mrs Mullaney's. The host was taken from the tabernacle and carried by the priests beneath a gold canopy all the way round the village, pausing for ceremonies at each wayside altar. Benediction was always at the post office. The congregation followed behind, some bearing the banners of their sodalities, and girls in white veils and dresses scattered rose petals from white boxes on the path before the host.[36]

The eldest of seven children, brought up by his mother on a small farm which she presumably ran with outside help as she was also the local primary school teacher, John was her dream of potential priesthood. His father lived some twenty miles away in the police barracks as Garda sergeant of the village. John's mother died when he was ten years old. The family moved to Cootehall to live with their father. From the reassuring ambiance of his mother's love, the boy was suddenly plunged into the impenetrable mystery of his father's overbearing presence.

John spent much of his life making up to his mother for turning down the vocation to the priesthood she had always had in mind for

....

35 Seamus Heaney, *Preoccupations, Selected Prose, 1968-1978*, London, Faber and Faber, 1980, p. 121.
36 John McGahern, *Love of the World*, Essays edited by Stanley van der Ziel, Faber and Faber, London, 2009, p. 138.

him. Preserving her memory is the task of his last book, *Memoir,* an autobiographical account of his childhood, published in 2005, a year before he died. The book is not just a biography; it is something of a commission. His mother had wanted him to become a priest.

> After the Ordination Mass I would place my freshly anointed hands on my mother's head. We would live together in the priest's house and she'd attend each morning Mass and take communion from my hands. When she died, I'd include her in all the Masses that I'd say until we were united in the joy of heaven.[37]

Memoir is the scripture of his mother's particular religion which her eldest son recorded as her evangelist. If God is love, and if the Church is meant to represent that love, then here is that love in its purest form. Woman and boy trace a path through their short life together, and it is the pattern and familiarity of that path — its persistent emotional echo — that McGahern wants us to experience and to understand. 'With her each morning, we went up the cinder footpath to the little iron gate, past Brady's house and pool and the house where the old Mahon brothers lived, past the deep, dark quarry and across the railway bridge and up the hill by Mahon's shop to the school, and returned the same way in the evening.' This sentence is repeated as a mantra several times verbatim throughout the book. Walking by his mother's side, especially after she returns from an absence which the children do not understand, but which is permeated with foreboding of her impending death, John felt 'safe in her shadow'.

> I am sure it is from those days that I take the belief that the best of life is life lived quietly, where nothing happens but our calm journey through the day, where change is imperceptible and the precious life is everything.

....
37   John McGahern, *Memoir*, London, Faber and Faber, 2005, p. 63.

Fintan O'Toole in his introduction to Eamon Maher's book *The Church and its Spire: John McGahern and the Catholic Question*, suggests that 'Catholicism matters to McGahern as a writer because it shapes his notion of what being a writer means. As with other male Irish writers of his generation, writing, for McGahern, is an alternative to the priesthood. This is not a mere biographical detail, though it is striking that in *Memoir* he seems to have felt some lasting guilt at breaking his promise to his mother that he would become a priest. It also shapes the nature of McGahern's literary career. Writing for him, was not a luxuriant escape from the rigours of a priestly life. It was, rather, even more rigorous, more demanding, more insistent on a life of total dedication. The austerity of his style is moral and spiritual as well as literary.'[38]

McGahern tries to explain to himself why so many young people in Ireland at that time chose the religious life or priesthood as their vocation:

> All through this schooling there was the pressure to enter the priesthood, not from the decent Brothers but from within oneself. The whole of our general idea of life still came from the Church, clouded by all kinds of adolescent emotions heightened by the sacraments and prayers and ceremonies. Still at the centre was the idea: in my end is my beginning. The attraction was not joy or the joyous altar of God; it was dark, ominous, and mysterious, as befits adolescence and the taking up, voluntarily, of our future death at the very beginning of life, as if sacrificing it to a feared God in order to avert future retribution. There was, too, the comfort of giving all the turmoil and confusion of adolescence into the safekeeping of an idea. [39]

....

38 Eamon Maher, *The Church and its Spire: John McGahern and the Catholic Question*, Columba Press, Dublin, 2011, pp. 12-13.

39 John McGahern, *Love of the World*, Faber, London, 2009, p. 142.

IV

Then Came the 60s

The power of religion peaked in the 1950s by which time the Catholic Church had become a lazy monopoly, the legacy of which is proving to be its greatest burden. The decline in the authority and pre-eminent position of the Catholic Church, the rise of secularism and the beginnings of the effort to dismantle legislative and constitutional support for a Catholic ethos can be traced to the early 1960s.[40]

'The Sixties', as they have come to be known, describe nostalgically for some a worldwide countercultural revolution; for others, a longing for return to the security of the 1950s away from 'that hideous decade'. Whatever way you look at them 'the swinging sixties' knocked the old order off its perch. Young people broke free from the social constraints of the previous half century and began to express themselves, often in extreme deviation from all prescriptive norms.

By the end of the 1950s, war-ravaged Europe had largely completed its reconstruction and had initiated an economic boom. World War II had brought about a levelling of social classes. The remnant of an old feudal gentry system was disappearing. There was a major expansion of the middle classes in European countries and many working-class families in the West could afford televisions, fridges, washing machines and motor cars. Such gadgetry gave freedom from the drudgery of daily chores and promoted prosperity, upward mobility, and self-reliance. The sixties bred a virus that eventually proved fatal to the 1950s world of Catholic Ireland.

40   Daithí Ó Corráin, Ibid., p. 727.

Why call it a virus? Because a virus is a small infectious agent that replicates itself only inside the living cells of other organisms. In itself it is nothing. The virus hardly exists until it gets stuck into something living and already existing. An organism at the edge of life, the virus appears negligible, peripheral, unremarkable, until it inserts itself into you as its host. Before you know where you are it begins to dismantle and destroy you. Once established within, it can infect all kinds of life forms which gave it existence in the first place. But only if you allow it to, if you harbour within you the deficiencies which give it free play. In other words, the host organism is partly responsible for its own demise. Viruses are found in every type of ecosystem, and are the most numerous type of biological entity. Immune responses against them can be produced artificially, if they don't already exist naturally in your make-up. But, if we are too complacent, or if we suffer from immune deficiency, then viruses can create a chronic infection.

Having become all too familiar with the Human Immunodeficiency Virus (HIV) which hit the planet devastatingly in the 1960s, we can use this familiar mechanism as a metaphor to illustrate the way in which viruses attacked the institutional church in Ireland from the 1960s onwards. Without going into too much technical detail about the nature and extent of our 'immune deficiency' let me exchange the all too familiar letters: HIV into realities with the same initial letters: the Hippie Movement, Information Technology and Vatican II. These three produced the human immunodeficiency which lodged deep inside the structures of society and caused them to topple.

The Hippie Movement

The 'hippie' movement began in the United States, it was said, and later spread to other places around the world. In fact it began much earlier and elsewhere. 'Make Love not War' was one of its catch cries. Young people were no longer prepared to obey their elders and be coerced into joining armies and fighting wars such as had destroyed previous generations.

Twice in the first half of twentieth century the youth of the world had become cannon fodder for their elders. Protesting the US military involvement in Vietnam, for instance, rightly or wrongly, came to be associated with the hippie movement.

The Woodstock Music and Art Festival in Bethel, New York and the Summer of Love in San Francisco epitomised the hippie ethos which included harmony with nature, communal living, artistic experimentation - particularly in music - and widespread use of recreational drugs, all of which, of course, undermined a prevailing Victorian ethos

The Woodstock Festival itself began on August 15, 1969 with half a million people waiting patiently on a dairy farm 80 miles from New York for the three-day music festival to begin. Billed as 'An Aquarian Experience: 3 Days of Peace and Music', the epic event became synonymous with countercultural movements of the 1960s.

Initially it was to be held at Howard Mills Industrial Park in Wallkill, New York. Town officials got spooked, however, and backed out of the deal, passing a law that eliminated any future possibility of holding such an event on their turf. Woodstock Ventures explored a few other venues, but none materialised. Finally, just a month ahead of the scheduled concert, a 49-year-old dairy farmer, Max Yasgur, offered to rent them part of his land in the White Lake area of Bethel, New York, surrounded by the Catskill Mountains. The four frantic partners jumped at the opportunity and paid the asking price. Over 500,000 people arrived to hear the most notable musicians and bands of the era, and in the ensuing mayhem, hippie ideals of love and fellowship gained worldwide traction.

A year earlier, what was billed as 'The Summer of Love' drew some 75,000 young people to the San Francisco streets. The gathering at the Haight-Ashbury district turned America into a new age. The Summer of Love 'bred a new kind of music —acid rock— put barbers out of business, traded clothes for costumes, advertised psychedelic drugs as doorways to the sacred, and revived the outdoor gatherings of a Messianic Age'.[41]

....

41   Sheila Weller, 'Suddenly that Summer', *Vanity Fair*, 1 July 2012.

These two events made headlines the world over and are credited with initiating a liberation movement which had actually begun in Ireland half a dozen years earlier as I am about to explain.

The first *Fleadh Cheoil* (meaning 'festival of [traditional] music') took place in Mullingar in 1951. Organised by *Comhaltas Ceoltoiri Eireann*, it was such a success they decided to hold the same event in 1963 in the same Westmeath town where the movement had been founded twelve years previously.

Survivors of that tumultuous weekend, where the youth of Ireland, growing in confidence and carelessness, gathered for music, drink and fornication, have often talked about their mid-summer night's dream, but few were able to describe its real impact. One eye-witness account has recalled: 'As a nine-year-old boy, I can still remember my mother and father talking animatedly about the mayhem surrounding us that Sunday, June 2, 1963, as the family car - a Triumph Herald my father must have bought in the throes of a mid-life crisis - made its way over the canal bridge and, with agonising slowness, inched through the heaving crowds on Austin Friars Street that sunny afternoon. The streets were awash with drink, and although I didn't fully understand - as I had never experienced anything like it in my short, sheltered, Catholic life - I still remember the swaying throngs and the figures, girls and boys, lying against each other on the footpath outside the Lake County Hotel, as the sounds of fiddles, accordions and guitars rent the air. That Sunday, there was no chance that we would call, as we usually did, to The Ennell Café in the middle of the town, which was owned by my Aunt Kitty and Uncle Tommy. When we were finally released from the clutches of the fleadh mob, after about two hours creeping crablike through the hordes, and reached the Longford road, my father put the boot down and didn't stop until we reached Ardagh, where my grandparents lived on a small farm. I have no memory of the return journey, but being a cautious man, my father probably decided to stay the night, and it may be that the Pope's death the following day,

Monday, June 3, 1963 at precisely 7.49pm, excised the memory of the fleadh from public consciousness.'

What was unleashed was so controversial at the time that the establishment pretended it never happened. The revelry of between 80,000 and 100,000 visitors to Mullingar that weekend was reported in a restrained fashion by the national newspapers, which concentrated on the damage to public buildings, shops and the 'interference' with cars.

'After a hectic opening on Saturday, when the antics of an unruly mob threatened the event, the Fleadh Cheoil closed on a dignified note,' reported the *Irish Press*. While there were reports of teenagers sleeping on and under the dance platforms erected around the town and in the tents that 'mushroomed' in fields and open spaces, the national newspapers avoided any reference to the 'lovers lying along the banks of the Royal Canal' that encircles Mullingar. But the local newspaper, the *Examiner*, not given to hyperbole or sensational journalism, was truly appalled at what went on in the town over that long Whit weekend, and said so in bold capital letters under a headline: 'Disgraceful and unruly scenes in Mullingar'.

'The indications are that the 1963 Fleadh Cheoil will be used as a dateline in the history of the town,' said the opening paragraph. 'An element poured into Mullingar and started what some people like to term high-jinks, but the town would have been a much better place without the orgy which these people were responsible for, and many breathed a sigh of relief when the unruly element left town.' Without giving the gory details of the 'orgy', the paper referred to the 'bedlam and unseemly conduct' of 'beatniks, Teddy boys and girls and undesirables from God knows where' who took over the streets, running in ribbons, doing the conga and the twist. 'Most of them armed with bottles and glasses of drink, [they] continued their mad demonstrations all through the night and well into the morning' it said, concluding: 'It was no small group; their numbers went into the thousands.'

The *Irish Independent*, which for the previous six days had front page headlines about the 'Pontiff slowly dying', referred to the 'jeans-clad youth' and the 'boisterous scenes' that had engulfed the town. But by Monday: 'Gone were the unruly element which had threatened to bring the future [of the fleadh] into disrepute, and the town was given over to Irish songs, dancing and music.'

What had brought this so called 'element' suddenly flooding into Mullingar? It was as if some secret signal was transmitted that the fleadh was the place to get away from the stifling control of their parents and flaunt a newfound freedom under the very noses of the political, religious and social establishment.

Two people who did 'get it' and saw what happened at the Fleadh Cheoil for what it really was, but from very different perspectives, were the Bishop of Meath, Dr John Kyne and the poet John Montague. When the bishop, alongside the President of Ireland, Éamon De Valera,, officially opened the Fleadh Ceoil in Mullingar, which up until that moment was no more than an obscure music festival in the Irish midlands, neither had any idea what they were unleashing. The bishop watched with horror from his nearby palace as events unfolded, turning an orthodox Catholic country into a hotbed of lust. 'Many have commented on the unseemly behaviour of many young men and women,' he said in a statement to the *Examiner* the following week. 'One cannot ignore the fact that many young men and women chose to make this festival an occasion of sinful conduct, giving great scandal to decent people in the town... we can only hope and pray that such scenes will not be witnessed again in our Catholic community.'

One local member of Comhaltas Ceoltoiri Eireann, Seamus O Murchadha, who confessed to having played an 'active part in bringing the Fleadh Cheoil to Mullingar', was so overcome with shame at the debauchery around him that weekend, that he resigned his membership of the organisation forthwith.

Incongruously, what was later described as 'an orgy' happened against the backdrop of the lingering death of Pope John XXIII in Rome, a pontiff who had reigned for less than five years, but who had made a huge impression on the Church with the Vatican Council, and whose kindly visage, in colour gravure, adorned the walls of most Irish Catholic households of the time.

John Montague (1929–2016) articulated the significance of the fleadh in a poem called 'The Siege of Mullingar,' which was published in *Arena* magazine in the autumn of 1963. Montague perceptively evoked the twin themes of the dying Pope and the young people of Ireland throwing off the yoke of puritan Catholicism that had dominated the Republic from the beginning.

> At the Fleadh Cheoil in Mullingar
> There were two sounds, the breaking
> Of glass, and the background pulse
> Of music. Young girls roamed
> The streets with eager faces,
> Shoving for men, bottles in
> Hand, they rowed out a song:
> *Puritan Ireland's dead and gone,*
> *A myth of O'Connor and O Faolain.*
>
> In the early morning the lovers
> Lay on both sides of the canal
> Listening on Sony transistors
> To the agony of Pope John.
> Yet it didn't seem strange, or blasphemous,
> This ground bass of death and
> Resurrection, as we strolled along:
> *Puritan Ireland's dead and gone,*
> *A myth of O'Connor and O'Faolain.*[42]

42   John Montague, *Selected Poems*, Dublin, The Dolmen Press, 1982, p. 62.

In November of that same year 1963 John F. Kennedy was shot dead in Dallas as he drove in an open limousine in cavalcade through the city. The world's innocence and freedom of movement were traded for a nightmare of protection squads and security arrangements. Never again would celebrities travel in open carriages through waving throngs of adoring fans.

In August 1963, Martin Luther King said 'I have a dream' and walked through Washington with 200,000 people to demand human rights for all people in this world. He too was later assassinated in Memphis, Tennessee, in April 1968 at 39 years of age.

'Beatlemania' hit the planet in that same year, 1963. And who was the first to introduce them on television; none other than your host, Gay Byrne.

Vatican II

The three great disasters of the twentieth century - according to one venerable monk in our community - were Hitler, De Valera and John XXIII. The Vatican Council which sent shivers down the spine of many a conservative Catholic, was a source of hope and expectation for countless others. This Second Vatican Council (1962-65) was perhaps the largest meeting in the history of the world. A gathering of over 2,000 Catholic priests, bishops, and cardinals from all over the planet met in Rome four autumns in a row, eight weeks at a time. Their average age was 60. Between the opening and closing dates 11th October, 1962 to 8th December, 1965, 253 of them died and 296 were added to their number. Between deaths, departures and new arrivals, it is estimated that a total of 2,860 attended part or all of the four periods. Between *periti* (the name given to those expert theologians who came to advise the bishops), journalists, observers, and guests, there were always at least 7,500 people present in Rome at any given time because of Vatican II. All were there to debate the nature of the Roman Catholic belief system.

In contrast to previous councils, 116 different countries were represented: 36% of these came from Europe; 34% represented the

Americas; 20% came from Asia and Oceania; 10% were from Africa. Only 750 bishops participated in Vatican I, and at The Council of Trent, the least well attended of all, only 29 bishops attended the opening ceremonies. Even at the largest sessions of this famous Tridentine Council, the number of voting members rarely exceeded 200.

From the very outset of Vatican II a war was waged. 'Nobody expected that almost as soon as the council opened two groups of leaders, both relatively small, would emerge from among those thousands of bishops, and that the rest of the bishops would have to judge between the two sides not only on a number of specific issues but also on a general orientation of the council.'[43]

To understand the context of this monster meeting we have to situate it in what has been termed the Catholic Church's 'long nineteenth century.' This contentious period, as far as Catholicism was concerned, dated from the French Revolution to the end of the pontificate of Pius XII in 1958. It also has to be seen in terms of the rise of Socialism and Communism in the first half of the twentieth century, and the traumatic experiences of World War II, less than two decades before the council began. Finally and more immediately still, there was the Cold War and the Cuban Missile Crisis which threatened the planet with nuclear annihilation.

Perhaps in sympathy with the character of the Pope who started it, the council adopted a new tone of respectful dialogue unheard of in previous councils which blasted enemies and condemned heretics, firing anathemas on all cylinders against pagans, infidels and schismatics.

Several overarching concerns dominated discussion. Most importantly, how the Church would deal with change? Two imperatives held sway: if they adulterated, altered or withheld anything of the original message of Jesus Christ, the Church would lose its soul, its very reason for existence. And yet, on the other hand, the Church would have to recognise that the message of Jesus Christ is not an abstraction above and beyond

---

43 John W. O'Malley, *What Happened at Vatican II*, The Belknap Press of Harvard University Press, Cambridge, Massachusetts, 2008, p. 290.

the human beings who first received it, or the human beings who have interpreted and passed it on through the centuries. The message entered the historical process, and by so doing it must, to some extent, become subject to change. By definition a transcendent message, it also by definition is meant for men and women of all times and cultures and so must be made meaningful for them.[44]

Two camps fell on either side of this important divide. Conservatives defended aggressively the 'no change' policy. Progressives were influenced by new philosophies of history and theories of the development of doctrine throughout history. Words like *aggiornamento* and *ressourcement* became catch cries for the second group, synonyms for change; and in the ears of the conservatives, euphemisms for renaissance and reformation. Many were in favour of a 'return to the sources,' dumping all the accretions which had gathered like barnacles on the side of the ship in between. So the battle was fought in depth and in detail and, as a result, the final texts, which had to be voted by the council as a whole, were always going to be a compromise between two points of view. Each side of the debate could read each sentence of the final texts as a triumph for their point of view. Those coming after them could thereby provide minimalist or maximalist interpretations of each word according to their particular preferences.

There was no doubting the interpretation of the Archbishop of Dublin, John Charles McQuaid. 'You may have been worried, he told his congregation at the Pro-cathedral on his return from Rome, 'by much talk of changes to come. Allow me to reassure you. No change will worry the tranquillity of your Christian lives.'[45]

But the deed had been done and the doubt had been sown. The very fact that discussions had taken place at all gave people the impetus to continue these discussions in their own, less prestigious but none the less impassioned exchanges. Among the more difficult challenges at

44 Ibid. p. 299.
45 Quoted by John Cooney, *John Charles McQuaid, Ruler of Catholic Ireland*, O'Brien Press, Dublin 1999, p. 371.

the time was how Irish Catholics and their leaders would respond to the far-reaching alterations in liturgy, theology, church governance and ecumenism promoted by the council.

Since 1850, a hundred years earlier, the Irish Catholic Church had been rigidly authoritarian in its governance, cautious if not hostile towards the modern world, conversionist in its stance towards Protestants, heavily Marian in its devotional emphasis, devoid of a scriptural tradition in either scholarship or popular piety, and strongly inclined to emphasise the externals of religious practice over any kind of interior spirituality. In all of these areas Vatican II pulled strongly in the opposite direction, insisting on a major role for the laity in church governance, finding much good in the modern world, encouraging respectful dialogue with other churches in a common effort towards Christian unity, focusing devotion much more on Christ than on Mary, stressing the importance of interior spirituality, and grounding both theology and popular piety in the scriptures.[46]

Vatican II was a crowbar dislodging the monolith on which many Roman Catholics had based their religious faith. Certain fundamental truths were altered in ways that put into question the whole operation. 'We were told as children, people in Ireland thought or said, that we shouldn't waste our time making friends with Protestants. They were a poor investment in friendship. We were going to be forever in heaven, while they were going to go to hell for all eternity.' Roman Catholics had been forbidden to take part in dialogue with other Christians, now they were being encouraged to engage with people of different denominations, other religions, or none at all. Where was the easily learned adage: '*Extra Ecclesia nulla salus*', which slipped so smugly and trippingly from the tongue: 'Outside the Catholic Church, no salvation.' Now we were being asked to call 'separated sisters and brothers' the very ones who had been heretics, apostates, pagans and proselytisers the year before?

46   John W. O'Malley, *What Happened at Vatican II*, The Belknap Press of Harvard University Press, Cambridge, Massachusetts, 2008.

The 'laity' (hideous word in any language) found themselves propagandised and promoted beyond all expectation. Lay people were the ones who really mattered, according to the Council: prophets, priests and kings from baptism no less. Consecrated religious people who had thought they were a cut above the rest in the kingdom of God, found out from the documents of Vatican II that they were no better than any ordinary lay person. Many left and got married.

Allowing the sacred Latin texts of the Mass, which Catholics had been brought up to view as divinely instituted and immutable, to be translated into vernacular languages had a disturbing and dislocating effect. Nothing would ever again be sacrosanct. Knowing what was being said at Mass in the banalities of your own language removed the aura and mystique of the familiar though inscrutable Latin formulae.

The sexual revolution meant that many religious and priests felt they had been duped. They had bought into a theory of purity and sacrificed their sexuality to false notions of human perfection. Far from being sinful and dangerous, their sexuality was one of the most beautiful gifts of humankind and they had been persuaded to sacrifice it in favour of a state which was now being questioned both psychologically and spiritually. Far from being an exalted superiority, celibacy and virginity were now perceived as stunted and futile. Not only were they of no particular value from a spiritual point of view but they were being portrayed as emasculation from a human point of view.

What Roman Catholics experienced in the second half of the twentieth century was a double earthquake: the Vatican Council and the Sexual Revolution. The gap at that point was too wide between the world being opened and the one being left behind. John McGahern put it neatly: 'Ireland is a peculiar society in the sense that it was a nineteenth century society up to about 1970 and then it almost bypassed the twentieth century.'

The straw that broke the camel's back was the Encyclical of Pope Paul VI, *Humanae Vitae*, subtitled 'On the Regulation of Birth,' promulgated on 25th July, 1968. This document re-affirmed traditional teaching of the Roman Catholic Church on abortion, contraception and other issues pertaining to human life, as well as reaffirming the Catholic Church's traditional view of marriage and marital relations. It prohibited of all forms of artificial contraception.

Ireland was already out of earshot. There was not much point in trying to close the door of the stable when the horse had already bolted. Even nursery rhymes had changed their tune.

> There was an old woman
> Who lived in a shoe
> She didn't have any children
> She knew what to do.

Information Technology

Here is a story that tells you all that needs to be known in this context about 'information technology'. My mother came to Ireland from America in 1936. She came by boat, on the Cunard line. Every single person in America at the time knew that the King of England, Edward VIII, was having an affair with a divorced woman, Mrs Wallis Simpson. It was all over the newspapers, with photographs of the pair bedecking the tabloid press. In Ireland, and indeed England, when my mother arrived, nobody knew about any of it. It was a secret. The government had forbidden the press to publish this news. The Prime Minister of Great Britain, Winston Churchill, had declared the news to be dangerous to national security, and the press obeyed his moratorium. When my mother began to ask people at parties in Dublin what they thought about the affair between the King of England and Wallis Simpson they thought she was off her head. Being a conscientious Catholic she asked a Jesuit priest whether it was libel, detraction or scandal that she was telling people here what was common knowledge in America but completely unknown in this country. 'I'm not quite sure which it is,' he said, 'but it's very interesting. Tell me more.'

We were an island. As far as information was concerned, we were cut off, controlled, manageable. The authorities could filter through whatever information they chose to divulge. Sixty years later in 1997, if Lady Diana Spencer could have enjoyed similar protection from paparazzi and publicity she might still be alive. The ways in which news is disseminated, information technology, has augmented exponentially. In a world of text, Twitter and Tik Tok, anything done by anyone on the planet, if considered 'newsworthy,' can be transmitted worldwide in seconds. Such prurient immediacy took time to develop but it was one of the seminal causes of cultural change.

Radio Éireann, first transmitted in 1926, reinforced a Catholic ethos. In 1950, for instance, the daily broadcast of the Angelus on RTÉ was introduced at the prompting of John Charles McQuaid, Archbishop of Dublin. Telefís Éireann on the other hand, inaugurated on New Year's Eve 1961, undermined the Catholic status quo from the outset. Oliver James Flanagan, TD for the Laois-Offaly constituency from 1943 to 1987, held famously that 'there was no sex in Ireland before television'.

Many people in Ireland learnt most of what they knew about what was going on in the world around them from *The Riordans*, the popular TV serial directed by Lelia Doolan, which ran for 15 years on RTÉ from 1965 to 1979. It was named after the central family, two middle-aged parents, Tom and his wife Mary Riordan, together with their oldest son, Benjy and his siblings. The show stopped most of the country in its tracks for one hour every Sunday evening of their lives, Bingo and Church devotions were rescheduled to accommodate the compelling alternative.

All this might seem strange in an era of multiple choice TV channels, Netflix and boxsets, but with little else to do on dark Sunday winter evenings and no other competing channels available, the compulsive nature of this second Irish RTÉ television drama serial can hardly be exaggerated. It portrayed real life in rural Ireland, covering a period of transition from an agrarian, protectionist stance in the early 1960s to membership of the European Economic Community and a rapidly changing rural economy in the 1970s. At the height of its popularity, 1.2 million viewers (a third of the population of the country in that year) attended Benjy and Maggie's wedding on screen.

The programme also tackled many 'conservative versus liberal' issues. Its first episodes coincided with the coming into force of the *Succession Act* which for the first time granted to the wife of a farmer an automatic right of succession to the family farm, so removing the danger that after her husband's death she could be left with nothing, the property having been willed to a total stranger. Banks until the 1970s would not allow a wife to open a bank account without the approval of her husband. Conservatives had suggested that the new Act, which had been pushed through in the face of opposition by the then Minister for Justice, Charles Haughey, would undermine the traditional family. What if a farmer's marriage was to break up? Liberals, on the other hand, argued that the reform was one of social justice and a long-overdue recognition of the rights of farmers' wives.[47] The Riordans took the bull by the horns, as it were.

The 'behind the bushes' episode, (in which the married Benjy, played by Tom Hickey, is seen coming out from the bushes with Colette Comerford played by Deirdre Lawless) resulted in several prominent town councils expressing their concern. A letter of complaint, preserved in the RTÉ archives, from twenty Clonmel parents accuses Benjy Riordan of 'joining the jet set and giving very bad example' kissing and flirting with Colette. Other frustrated viewers wrote angrily to RTÉ demanding that 'whatever was going on behind the bushes at Leestown, County Kilkenny, should be brought right out into the open immediately so that everybody can see what's going on!'

But nothing to the uproar when it was revealed that Benjy's wife, Maggie, for medical reasons, because she could not risk having a second pregnancy, had taken the decision to use 'the pill.' This caused considerable controversy and criticism from 'family values' organisations.

47   Finola Kennedy, *Cottage to Crèche: Family Change in Ireland* (Dublin: Institute of Public Administration, 2001) p. 302.

It is ironic that the year 1979, which saw the introduction of legalised contraceptives into Ireland, was the year that Ireland's most popular soap was suddenly axed from the RTÉ schedule. Wesley Burrows, who was primarily responsible for the script, was less concerned about the axing than about the use of the term 'soap' to describe his creation. 'Soap,' in his view, is the way to describe 'a bad serial'.

Gay Byrne, the name synonymous with Irish radio and television, joined Radio Éireann in 1958 and was on our TV screens from the moment RTÉ hit the tarmac in Donnybrook, Dublin 4. First host of *The Late Late Show* from 1962 to 1999 he turned it into one of the world's longest-running chat shows. Gay Byrne had worked in England with the BBC and Granada Television, where else would he have learned the tricks of the trade, ending up with *The Late Late Show*, that 'purveyor of filth' as Michael Browne, the Bishop of Galway described the programme. First aired in July 1962 as a six-week summer filler, producer Tom McGrath intended it to be light entertainment, full of informal chat and easy banter; an Irish version of America's *The Tonight Show*.

Gay Byrne had other ideas. Brash, slick and far smarter than he pretended to be, he quickly turned the show into a mirror of a changing society. It became the forum where controversial topics such as the influence of the Catholic Church, contraception, AIDS, homosexuality, abortion, and divorce could be openly discussed. Until the arrival of this programme, matters of personal intimacy were virtually unheard of as topics of public discussion in Ireland. Now Irish broadcasting in the 1960s and 1970s reflected the clash of ideas between elements of traditional rural Catholic society and new liberal ideas coming from the United States, Britain and Catholicism itself through the reforms of the Second Vatican Council.

The Bishop and the Nightie

One evening, Gay Byrne picked a married couple from the audience, Richard and Eileen Fox from Terenure in Dublin, and asked each of them a series of questions while the other was out of earshot. One of the questions related to the colour of Eileen's nightie on the first night of their honeymoon. Richard said it was transparent, while Eileen said she wasn't wearing any.

Thomas Ryan, Bishop of Clonfert in Galway, issued an immediate complaint to the *Sunday Press*, which gave it front-page treatment the following morning. The bishop, in his sermon at eight o'clock Mass in St Brendan's Cathedral, Loughrea, urged his congregation to register protests 'in any manner you think fit, so as to show the producers in Irish television, that you, as decent Catholics, will not tolerate programmes of this nature'. Letters to the newspapers continued for weeks, including one which suggested that people from West Cork wore corduroys in bed on their honeymoons.

The Nightie and the Bishop

One man became synonymous with the destruction of the image of priesthood in Ireland and the decline in the fortunes of the Catholic Church. He was a high-profile personality in the 1970s and 1980s, a media star as well as a prince of the Church. It was he, among the bishops of Ireland who introduced Pope John Paul II at the Mass for young people in Galway in 1979. By the mid-1980s, his celebrity had reached such heights that RTÉ offered him a slot for a one night hosting of the *Saturday Live* chat show. He regaled his audience with 'come-all-ye' songs and boasted of knowing 400 ballads off by heart.

After a succession of severe-looking cardinals and bishops, Eamonn Casey brought the swinging sixties with him to Ireland when he was appointed Bishop of Kerry in 1969. Growing up himself in Co. Kerry in the 1930s, he could scarcely have imagined the role he would one day play in the Church's hierarchy and in the decline and fall of Catholicism in Ireland.

Casey was the bridge between the fusty and reserved old-world hierarchy, and the modern media world of bishops in the sixties. With his populist touch and crowd-pleasing manner, he was standard-bearer for the new-look Church of the future. For the Irish media, Eamonn

Casey was the gift that kept on giving. He was pure show business: fast cars, fine wines, that engaging smile which lit up the studio.

During his years as Bishop of Kerry and later, as Bishop of Galway, Casey was one of Uncle Gaybo's favourite stalwarts. He would burst into the studio gleefully recounting that he had made it up from Kerry or across from Galway in his powerful BMW, in less time than many Dublin commuters took to get themselves home from work. He boasted that he could dance like Fred Astaire, liked to eat in fancy restaurants, and would have liked to be a racing driver in another career. Two decades later this carefully contrived image would come crashing down. And Gay Byrne could never have imagined that his most successful guest would be responsible for the most talked-about *Late Late Show* ever broadcast.

In 1993, a young American woman, Annie Murphy, came on to his show to tell the world about her sexual affair with the bishop, which produced their son, Peter. She had kept the affair secret for 18 years until the bishop's son, (with whom he later reconciled), came of age and was unwilling to continue the subterfuge. By then Eamonn Casey had fled to South America via Rome where he had handed the Pope his resignation, ahead of the story breaking in the media.

In 1974, Annie Murphy was 25 and getting over nasty divorce proceedings when her father, a distant cousin of Bishop Casey, sent her to stay with the newly-appointed bishop. During his time in Kerry, not only did he have a 'palace in Killarney', he also had a secluded holiday home on the coast near the village of Annescaul on the Dingle peninsula. The hunting lodge, once owned by the Earl of Listowel, was where he brought Annie Murphy on holiday. They became lovers. Annie Murphy's account of the affair in her book, *Forbidden Fruit*, said to have been ghosted by the well-known writer and former Catholic priest, Peter de Rosa, is almost the stuff of sex comedy: 'There stood the bishop, my love, without clerical collar or crucifix or episcopal ring, without covering of any kind. The great showman had unwrapped himself. I witnessed a great hunger. This was an Irish famine of the flesh.'

Within a short time, Annie was accompanying 'Bishop Eamonn' on social occasions. In October 1973, she became pregnant and their son Peter was born on 31st July, 1974. Some months later, Annie Murphy left Ireland.

This news was not well received in Ireland on her return trip to tell her story and promote her book. Such was especially the case on *The Late Late Show*. Neither Gay Byrne nor his audience were ready at that point for the smashing of idols that had only begun. Annie Murphy quoted Mark Twain: 'Every man is a moon and has a dark side which he turns toward nobody.' This was true not only of her erstwhile lover, but for anyone placed on the altar as an idol.

In light of the scandals that followed, many wondered where was the harm in a tryst involving two consenting adults. The 'disgrace' of the bishop fathering a child soon paled to insignificance as sex abuse scandals engulfed and discredited the Irish Church. Nonetheless, when the time comes to write the definitive history of the declining influence of the Catholic Church in twentieth century Ireland, Casey's departure will certainly mark a pivotal moment. For many Irish people, it was the beginning of a series of punishing revelations that discredited the Church which they were brought up to believe would always do the right thing. The litany of evil deeds and subsequent hypocrisy was as lengthy as it was devastating. The definitive crack had appeared in the monolithic edifice which was the Catholic Church throughout the twentieth century. Nothing would ever be the same again. The other scandals which followed would be far more lurid and obscene, but the first is nearly always the worst. A rider was attached to *Humanae Vitae*: 'Always carry a condom just in Casey.' Eamonn would always be remembered. The scales had fallen from people's eyes and everyone began to realise that the king had no clothes.

The Good Friday Disagreement

Nothing describes more graphically the move from the nineteenth to the twenty-first century in Ireland, than a ninety-year-old struggle for the right to have a pint on Good Friday.

The Intoxicating Liquor Act, introduced in 1927, prohibited the sale of all alcoholic drink on Christmas Day, Good Friday and St Patrick's Day. The St Patrick's Day clause was repealed in 1960 so visitors coming to Ireland could refresh themselves in pubs across the country on our national holiday.

When the Licensed Vintners and Grocers' lobby agitated for a relaxation of the licensing laws on Sundays in 1948, the bishops' approach to their petition was haughtily disdainful:

> Largely in deference to our wishes the Bill was decisively rejected, and we were under the impression that our guidance in this matter, so intimately connected with ... public morals, was accepted, and we expected that no further attempt would be made to modify the existing civil law forbidding the sale of intoxicating drink on the Lord's Day.

Given that they had already pointed out in 1948 that a change in legislation would lead to 'a grave increase in intemperance and to other moral evils', their lordships were decidedly aggrieved that 'it has, therefore, become necessary for us to set forth our views on this matter once more'. Interestingly, they had recourse to State law to support what was a Catholic precept. The tone and the approach of the bishops in this exchange are petulant, condescending, paternalistic and authoritarian. That tone would change over the century, as would the wheedling tone of the Licensed Vintners and Grocers. In time such attitudes and demeanours would change on both sides. In 1950 there was no doubting either the authority or the power wielded by the bishops in all matters including the right to a pint. Agitation from the Licensed Vintners and Grocers' lobby came to an abrupt end and several years passed before sufficient courage was mustered to re-open negotiations.

On the 4th July, 1978, I was in a court room in Bray, Co. Wicklow. My mother had been run down by a truck in Greystones, Co. Wicklow and had been hospitalised. She was due to appear in court that day to press charges against the driver of the truck. We had been told that the case before ours would not take long and that my mother would not be kept waiting. As it happened, the case before ours took the whole morning, but it wasn't to be missed

A garda had discovered a group of men at the bar in the Royal Starlight Hotel on Main Street, Bray drinking pints on Good Friday. This was no off-beat sheebeen, we were reminded; this was a highly reputable premises. There has been an hotel on the site of the Royal Hotel in Bray since 1776 and it was a well-known and popular venue both locally and internationally. Notable visitors and guests in the past included Percy Bysshe Shelley, William Makepeace Thackeray, Sir Arthur Conan Doyle and Charles Dickens. During his visit to Bray, Dickens had heard of Augusta Magan, who lived at Corke Lodge in Shankill, whose eccentric and reclusive life are said to have inspired his creation of Miss Havisham, in *Great Expectations*.

The group apprehended by the overly conscientious and imprudent garda had hired a well-known solicitor who knew how to handle the law and rescue clients even when blatantly culpable. You were allowed to have a drink on Good Friday if you were staying at a hotel and a meal was being served. All the clients caught red-handed at the bar had signed the hotel register and booked themselves in for the night immediately after their apprehension. The policeman who had apprehended them was being cross-examined by the solicitor while a rowdy audience of friends and well-wishers were packed into the gallery cheering the prosecutor and booing the witness.

The policeman persisted and assured the judge that there was no meal being served on the premises.

'How many rooms are there in the hotel?' he was being bullied by the solicitor.

He had no idea. His questioner looked dumbfoundedly towards the gallery.

'And while you were so conscientiously doing your duty on Good Friday, 24th March, 1978, did you bother to inspect any of those other rooms in the hotel?'

He had not.

And how could you possibly know, in that case, that there wasn't a meal being served in one of those rooms?

[Hoots of laughter and tumultuous applause from his fans above]

Needless to say the miscreants got off with a warning never to be found drinking on Good Friday again. They admitted to a firm purpose of amendment and left the court room in hysterics.

Where would the courage to take up the cudgels in this struggle for human rights be found? You guessed it: Limerick yet again. 'The Good Friday closure controversy' or 'Good Friday Disagreement' refers to the 2010 court case which saw publicans in Limerick apply to be exempted from the prohibition on selling alcohol on Good Friday that year. The case came about following the scheduling of a 2009-2010 Celtic League Rugby match between Leinster and Munster in Thomond Park on 2nd April, 2010. The match had sold out by the time the court application took place, and was due to kick off at 20:05. Television rights had already been agreed.

Vintners argued that Limerick publicans stood to lose revenue valued at around €6 million or as much as €10 million if they were prevented from opening for business as normal on that historic day. It was considered a landmark case before it had even begun. The State and the Garda Síochána were against changing the law. Long story short, the vintners won and pubs were permitted to do business on Good Friday in the Republic of Ireland for the first time since 1927 (though only in Limerick). The victory was hailed as an 'historic ruling' and 'a watershed' in Church-State relations. Mayor Kiely told the religious and anti-drinkers to 'get real' and invited people from across Ireland to come to the city of Limerick to drink on the day.

Fast forward to Good Friday 30th March, 2018. Irish bars are to open their doors for the first time in over 90 years for a Good Friday booze-up. People said they were going to spend the whole day in a pub to mark the occasion. Senator Billy Lawless, who is an independent, introduced The Intoxicating Liquor (Amendment) Bill and which he said was needed to make Ireland a 'forward-thinking' country ... It was another progressive step in Ireland's long journey in the separation of Church and State. The media took up his cause: 'In the eyes of many foreigners and quite a few natives too, drink and the Irish go together like gin and tonic,' one newspaper article began. 'There is really no doubt that as a nation, we do have a reputation abroad for being accomplished swillers of beer, and sinkers of spirits.'

Queues formed outside pubs in Ireland as the 90-year ban on serving alcohol on Good Friday was lifted. Some punters eager to experience the novelty of ordering a pint on the holy day were lined up outside early opening bars from 7am. A barman spoke to reporters: 'They are all excited to come in and work, they want to be part of history because of us being the first bar to actually serve drink at 7am,' he said. 'They all want to get their picture in the paper.' VFI Chief Executive, Padraig Cribben, said: 'The extra day's business is a welcome boost to the pub trade. It is estimated that Good Friday will generate over €40 million in sales for pubs throughout the country.' So the shackles are off! Headlines in the papers told us: 'Good Friday finally upgrades to Great Friday and may even become our National Drinking Day.' A new craft beer called 'For Your Sins' was launched by Five Lamps Brewery; lest it be suggested that all religious sensibility had been abandoned, if your name happened to be Jesus, Mary or Joseph, you were entitled to a free cocktail at the Adelphi on Abbey Street.

V

Three Weddings and a Funeral

It was definitely a matter of two tribes in County Limerick, and rarely did the Romeo and Juliet syndrome disturb the rigid protocols of species preservation. From the Protestant point of view it was a question of not letting the side down, of not marrying beneath your station. The Penal Laws, obviously, when previously in force, helped the Irish Parliament, which was entirely Protestant, to discourage, without actually banning, Catholicism. Catholics were denied political power, which depended on land ownership. These laws were less effective than intended by those passing them. They were laxly enforced and, as we have seen in the case of my own family, Catholics were able to hold many large estates, which they did with the connivance of Protestant friends and neighbours.

From the Catholic perspective, on the other hand, there was a long history of stigmatisation and punishment for those seen to be collaborators or paramours of the colonisers. There was also the attempt by Rome to discourage all such liaisons. *Ne Temere* the decree issued by Pope Pius X in 1908, named for its opening words, which mean, 'lest rashly', made clear the repercussions for anyone who might dare to marry someone who was not a Catholic. If you do have the temerity, then read the small print: a Catholic, whether practising or lapsed, to marry someone of another religion in a marriage recognised by the Catholic Church, must get a dispensation, granted only on condition that any resultant children be baptised and brought up as Catholics. The non-Catholic partner must submit to religious education with the aim of converting them to Catholicism. Both the Catholic and non-Catholic spouse must pledge during the wedding ceremony to raise their children as Catholics. This decree was in force until 1970.

Three spectacular upsets to such unwritten taboos were recorded in County Limerick during my lifetime.

Kilgobbin

Colonel Henry Wyndham-Quin, who wrote the book on Foxhunting in Limerick, belonged to one of the oldest families of ancient Celtic nobility. He became the fifth Earl of Dunraven and Mount-Earl when his cousin, the fourth earl, died without male issue. Henry's grandson, born in 1939, became the 7th Earl of Dunraven and Mount-Earl in 1965. Thady Wyndham-Quin, whose ancestors, the O'Quins, were chiefs of the Clan Hy Ifearnan in Co. Clare before being driven out by the O'Briens, resided at Adare Manor and owned extensive properties which his family had acquired towards the end of the seventeenth century. Thady, who was educated at Ludgrove School in England and at Le Rosey in Switzerland, was one of 500 people, mostly children, who contracted polio during the Cork epidemic in the summer of 1956. By the time the symptoms appeared, he had returned to school in Switzerland. In spite of having access to Swiss medical expertise, he was confined to a wheelchair for the rest of this life. He caused a sensation in Limerick when, in 1969 he married a Catholic. Geraldine McAleer was born in Dublin in 1942. She was the daughter of Sheila Byrne and Gerard Ward McAleer, a medical doctor from Dungannon, Co. Tyrone. Thady and Geraldine had a daughter Ana, but when Thady died at the age of 71 in 2011 with him died all the titles of one of those rare families of true Gaelic origin in the Irish peerage.

Rathmore

Martin Molony died on Monday, 10th July, 2017 at the age of 91. He and his brother Tim, who died in 1989, were top jockeys in their day. Statues of the two by Paul Ferriter can be seen at the entrance to Limerick racecourse. The Molony brothers recorded a unique triumph when Tim won the British jockey championship in 1949, with Martin as runner-up. But Martin was also champion jockey in Ireland that same year. He held this position as Ireland's champion jump jockey between 1946 and 1951. He won the Cheltenham Gold Cup on Silver Fame in 1951 and the Irish Grand National on three occasions. Acclaimed one of the most stylish riders of his generation, he is still the benchmark for young aspiring jump jockeys, 'one of the best in the history of the turf'.

At the age of 26, on 18th September, 1951, he had a serious fall on Bursary in Thurles. He crushed his skull and was in a coma for several days. When he recovered he was advised to give up racing. He retired to his home at Rathmore, where he farmed and bred horses, finding time to engage his passion for hunting with the Limerick Hounds. It was on the hunting field that he met Julia Hilton-Greene. To everyone's amazement they got married in 1960. In marrying Martin she had married not only a Roman Catholic but what might be regarded as a 'raving mad Catholic'. Martin was forever going to Mass, saying his prayers, thanking God for everything. People referred to him as 'Blessed Martin'. This would have been a reference to Martin de Porres, a Portuguese saint who was highly popular in Ireland at the time.

A seventeenth-century Peruvian lay brother of the Dominican order, Martin de Porres was the son of a Spanish nobleman and Ana Velázquez, a freed slave of African and native descent. He was canonised in 1962 by Pope John XXIII, so at this time he was still 'Blessed Martin' and on everybody's lips as the crowds were rooting for his full recognition as a saint. Such familiar jocosity was part of the banter between Catholics at the time, much in the same way that Martin Maguire, the very big man who owned the enormous flour mill in Limerick, the buildings of which can still be seen jutting out into the Shannon beyond Arthur's Quay, was nicknamed 'The Little Flower,' in oblique deference to Thérèse of Lisieux. Such jocose coded quips of Catholic conversation would have been lost completely in uncomprehending and perhaps disdainful Protestant society. Suffice it to say that Julia, who became a Catholic before her wedding, had certainly taken the plunge into an alternative culture. The day Julia was accepted into the Roman Catholic Church, having received every sacrament available bar ordination, the last rites and (as yet) the sacrament of marriage, Martin and she headed off on a romantic picnic together. Reclining among the wild flowers on the banks of Lough Gur, Julia was up for some time-honoured and customary kissing and cuddling. Martin was dumbfounded, awestruck at the sight of her. He told her he had never seen her look so beautiful. She asked him why at this moment? Because, he said, she was now in such a state of grace that, if she were to die on the spot, she would go straight to heaven.[48]

They lived at Rathmore and had five children. Then tragedy struck. Julia began to suffer from a muscle-wasting disease which confined her to a wheelchair for the last 40 years of her life. It was then that 'Blessed Martin' really came into his own. He looked after his beloved through all those years of relentless debilitation, which she bore with heroic patience until she passed away in 2016, a year before Martin himself did.

Kilfrush

The third sensation was the most colourful of the three. Kilfrush had been in the Gubbins family for 380 years. John Gubbins was Master of the Limerick Foxhounds from 1882 to 1887. Their stately home in Knocklong, Co. Limerick, had been built in 1825. When Francis Beresford Gubbins died in November 1930, the male line of Kilfrush Gubbins died out. He was survived by his wife Katherine, who died in 1959, and their only daughter, Maureen Frances. Maureen Gubbins was President of the Munster Branch of the Irish Horse Trials and Dressage Society. A keen horsewoman, she ran Kilfrush without a problem on her own.

The most flamboyant swashbuckling huntsman for the Limericks was Pat Hogan, otherwise known as P.P. If anyone knew everything about

---

48   I have this recollection on the authority of their son Peter Molony, who wrote to me in October, 2020. Peter came to school at Glenstal Abbey and was elected School Captain by his peers in 1985, the year I took over as Director of the school. In Department of Education speak, I was Co-Director as principal of the school, Tim McGrath was the other Co-Director as manager, and Jim Hegarty was, what the boys called Co-Co Director as vice-principal. Peter now runs the stud farm at Rathmore.

horses it was P.P. He began his riding career at the stables of Charlie Rodgers. As an amateur jockey he set a new non-professional record in 1942 by riding 32 winners out of 98 rides. The list of stables that made use of his talents is a 'Who's Who' of the racing world: Vincent O'Brien, Tom Draper, Paddy Sleator, W.T. O'Grady, to name but a few. He once cycled to Kilkenny, rode several winners, stayed overnight, then continued on to Carlow where he rode four point to point winners; on his way home he stopped off at Thurles where he rode two winners, one for Vincent O'Brien and the other on a horse called Revelry, which later won the Irish Grand National in 1947.

In the days when 'steeplechasing' really did mean a hell for leather dash across country between two church spires, P.P. was also champion. He won the Kildorrery to Buttevant classic of 1954, when seventy riders from six counties lined up at the start. A last minute ruling prevented him from being one of the Irish Equestrian team in the 1960 Olympics in Rome. Selected, he trained with the team for six months, until it was discovered that he had a trainer's licence which automatically debarred him from competing at the Olympics. He rode his last winner in 1971.

Widely acknowledged as one of the world's best judges of bloodstock, he advised on the purchase of over 200 winners. He could look at a horse and evaluate potential. This instinctual expertise assessing 'the look of a horse' was rare and recognised. He was taken all over the world by trainers and owners spotting talent. He once told Robert Sangster to spend $200,000 on an undistinguished-looking foal he had spotted in a field. Sangster obeyed, and the filly won three of her first six races. But the racing bargain of the twentieth century must be the 3,000 guineas P.P. paid at Newmarket for the yearling Rheingold. Nine winning races later, clocking up a European Stakes record of £357,000 in prize money, Rheingold was syndicated for over a million to stand as sire.

P.P. was also a rogue. His favourite pastime was hunting, and he spent many days with the Limericks in the countryside he knew like the back of his hand. Part of his job as 'huntsman' was to make life easier for lesser mortals, some out hunting for the first time. Whereas he was wonderfully kind to children, he was mischievous to unfortunates who had paid huge sums to go riding fashionably with the Limericks. Many of these were foreigners without much or any experience of horse riding. P.P. would gallop ahead to find the easiest way for others to follow the hounds, through gates, across fields, into rivers, over stone walls. If fences, as was often the case, had barbed wire on top, he could jump his horse leaning over with a secateurs to snip the wire as both he and the horse sailed through. Instead of finding the point in the river where a horse could cross without difficulty, he would make his own horse gallop towards the deepest part of the river, leaving a trail of hoof-marks behind so that followers would think they were being lead to where they should jump. At the last minute he would stop his own horse, retire behind a tree and watch with undisguised glee as the immaculately attired amateurs plunged into the river to be swept away downstream while their horses clambered to the far bank.

If you were a child on the hunt, as we were, he would look after you like an angel. Pat Smythe recalls in her book that she learned most of what she knew about foxhunting from P.P. when she went to Rathmore for the second half of her stay in Ireland. My sister, Louise, recalls visiting him in hospital in the 1980s: 'He was overjoyed to find someone he could manipulate. Before I knew it he'd hopped into my car and I drove him to Dermot Weld's yard in Kildare. On the way down I asked him what made him such an expert at spotting talent in a yearling (untried). He said, though he couldn't read or write, all he needed was to see the head and shoulders of a yearling being lead from the box and he could judge. Of course we all loved him, especially as kids.'

Anyway, P.P. married Maureen Gubbins in 1947 and they took up residence in Kilfrush, where they operated a horse breeding and training establishment. Her lawyers advised her not to let P.P. anywhere near her bank account or her family fortune. P.P. was up to the challenge. He could outfox lawyers and accountants. Stories circulated wildly.

Whenever Maureen left the house, P.P. would round up and sell half her cattle. On her return, if she summoned the lawyers and the accountants to drive around the land and count the cattle, they would travel by car from field to field on their computing expedition. Meanwhile, the bold Pat with the help of the farm staff would drive the cattle from one field to the next, so that the lawyers would be counting the same cows in one field which had just been driven there at top speed from the field beside. Eventually the ruse was detected. Several cows were found on their last legs panting from exhaustion from the marathon run throughout the estate. Other versions of the story had it that P.P. would sell the resident herd of mature animals and replace them with yearlings so the number would remain the same but the value would have decreased by whatever amount necessary to keep himself in pocket with the proceeds. Whether all this was true or an exaggerated version of some truth, it was part of the local legend and mythology.

Whatever the distinction between truth and legend, the facts remain: in 1969 John Mulcahy, an Irish-American, purchased Kilfrush and 230 acres of land for a sum in excess of 52,000 Irish pounds. The Irish Land Commission acquired the remaining land. Thus ended 300 years of Gubbins ownership.

A Tale of Two Castles
GLENSTAL

Glenstal Castle was built by Sir Matthew Barrington between 1833 and 1853. The first part of the castle was completed by 1839 by William Bardwell who chose the townland of Garranbane rather than Glenstal as it offered a better view of the Galtee Mountains and the surrounding countryside of south-east Limerick. This landscape is now dominated by a nineteenth-century 'Norman' castle pretending to be built in the twelfth century. The Barrington family had come to Ireland with Oliver Cromwell and were metal workers or clock makers. By the beginning of the nineteenth century they had acquired enough wealth to buy a baronetcy. Matthew's father, Sir Joseph, was the first to carry the title. Matthew obviously wanted to make an impression and perhaps suggest that his family lineage stretched back to the Norman conquests. So, he built his castle in the medieval style of the twelfth century and placed carved statues of Henry II of France and Eleanor of Aquitaine in the awning of the entrance doorway.

The grounds were designed as an earthly paradise. Some of the family even travelled to America to bring back trees which are some of the largest and most exotic this side of the Atlantic. Matthew's son Sir Charles Burton Barrington was born in 1848 and succeeded to his father's estates in 1890. This was a troubled time for such landlords. Tragic circumstances caused the estate to change hands. There are many versions of what happened. The grim facts are that his daughter Winifred was shot in an ambush at Coolboreen Bridge near Newport on Saturday the 14th May, 1921. The ambush was carried out by the IRA whose actual target was Captain Harry Biggs, a military officer who was District Inspector and head of the RIC station at Newport. Such a spectacular tragedy caused much sympathetic reporting about Winnie's friendly personality and her good relations with local people, even those known to be republican sympathisers.

A whole mythology began to grow up around Winnie Barrington, who was buried in the graveyard beside Abington Church. This was the site of the thirteenth-century Cistercian Abbey Owney. The headstone over her grave still movingly reads: 'Here lies all that could die of Winifred Frances Barrington.' Why was Winifred Barrington in the car with the British officer being targeted by the Irish revolutionaries? One version of the mythology suggests that there was 'a kind of romance' going on between Winnie and Captain Biggs.[49] This notion is dismissed by another historian who claims that Winnie couldn't have been flirting with a British officer because she had her eye on a local Irish lad called

49 Mark Tierney O.S.B., *Glenstal Abbey, A Historical Guide*, Glenstal Abbey Publications, 2009, p. 37.

Mick Hayes, who worked in some capacity for her father. Proof of this second theory centres upon an existing postcard which she sent to Mick Hayes from the Hotel du Parc in France while she was holidaying at Cannes. The card reads: 'I hope you are all grand and best wishes for 1921. It is very hot out here and lovely scenery but I am looking forward tremendously to returning to Ireland in March ... I'll ride up and see you directly I get home.'[50] The postcard shows a picture of the *Promenade de la Croisette* and Winnie has written under it 'We walk here in the morning, but I'd give anything for a ride!!'

If a young lady of Winnie Barrington's background and education happens to scrawl in 1921 on the front of an open postcard that she would 'give anything for a ride,' we cannot interpret this with any of the lurid and all-knowing consciousness of twenty-first century voyeurs. Such an innocent greeting to a groom who kept horses in the district around Glenstal can in no way suggest any hint of romance. If Boodley or Merry Atkinson had sent a card on their holidays in Switzerland to one of their favourite hounds in the kennel at Clonshire, it would have about the same significance.

My preferred version of the myth is as follows: Winnie was a feisty young woman. Captain John Regan, County Inspector for Police in Limerick City at the time, describes her in his memoir as 'brave as a lioness'.[51] She being an emancipated woman of her time wanted to drive a motor-car. Her parents were horrified and said that under no circumstances would a lady of her standing ever be seen behind the wheel of an automobile. Although such luxuries were a rarity in Ireland at the time, the Barringtons had two cars in Glenstal Castle. They promised her a compromise. If she wanted to travel by car they would send her to a finishing school in Paris where she could be taught how a young

....

50 Quoted in Brian P. Murphy OSB, *The Life and Tragic Death of Winnie Barrington*, Limerick, Papaver Editions, 2018.
51 John Regan, ed. Joost Augusteijn, *The Memoirs of John M. Regan*, 1909-1948, Dublin, 2007, p. 151.

lady might get into and get out of (one semester for each of these stylish movements) the passenger seat of an automobile.

The young lady was having none of it. She knew someone who owned such an automobile and she would arrange to have secret lessons from him. Captain Biggs, an English officer, was her designated tutor. She was hardly to know that he had been targeted by local freedom fighters. On the evening of the 14th May, 1921 Winifred and Biggs were returning to Glenstal by car from Killaloe. She was wearing the goggles and all the gear required at the time for drivers of a car, and no one imagined that a woman would be in that position. They were ambushed along the Newport road and she was killed. The attackers took her for Biggs and only realised later that she was dead and he still alive. Eventually he was also killed.

Speculation continues about Winnie Barrington, about the circumstances surrounding her death and about the person who killed her. No incontrovertible evidence has emerged to substantiate the many theories which have been put forward. There is enough evidence to keep anyone interested in spending their life in such research fully occupied. What cannot be denied is that a pseudo-Norman castle built at great expense and ingenuity as a Protestant paradise in Co. Limerick in the nineteenth century has become in the twenty-first century a Catholic Benedictine monastery which enjoys all the investment, energy and toil expended in its creation. How did this happen?

Sir Charles and Lady Barrington, with the rest of their family, left Glenstal to live in England on their Hampshire estate. Nothing could be done about their properties here until after the Civil War (1922-23) when Sir Charles offered Glenstal to the Irish Free State government as an official residence for the Governor-General. If the gift had been accepted, the President of Ireland might be living in Glenstal castle today. However, the offer was turned down as the estate was thought to be too expensive to run and too far from Dublin.

In 1926 Glenstal Castle was bought by a local priest and given to the Benedictine monks from Maredsous in Belgium to found a community.

Why were the monks invited? Two Murroe-born clergymen, John Harty, Archbishop of Cashel and Richard Devane, Professor of Church History at St Patrick's College, Thurles, wanted to find some appropriate future for the castle and estate which would also be of benefit to their home parish. They admired the influence of Benedictine monasteries on the continent and especially the Abbey of Maredsous in Belgium, where they knew the abbot of the time who was an Irishman.

Columba Marmion was born in Dublin on 1st April, 1858 to an Irish father (William Marmion) and a French mother (Herminie Cordier). Joseph Aloysius entered the Dublin diocesan seminary in 1874 and completed his theological studies in Rome. He was ordained a priest in 1881. His dream was to become a missionary monk in Australia, but he was won over by the liturgical atmosphere of the newly founded Abbey of Maredsous in Belgium, which he had visited on his return to Ireland after his ordination. In 1886 he entered Maredsous as a monk and became their third abbot in 1909. He died in 1923. It was in his honour that the monks of Maredsous founded a monastery in Ireland, dedicated to Saints Joseph and Columba. Marmion had been something of a best-selling author. His books on spirituality sold the world over. It was on the royalties from these that the monks of Maredsous were able to finance the foundation in Ireland.

Local people had never seen anything like the first monks who arrived. First of all they spoke French. Their hair was shaven like convicts. They wore black habits and hoods that looked like long dresses or spooky Hallowe'en costumes. One of the first pioneer monks was Mayol Lang, of diminutive stature, and another Omer Van Tours, who was double his size. On one occasion shortly after their arrival, the pair wandered off behind the castle to the hinterland woods. They got lost. Coming upon a local farmer they asked him how they might find their way back to the castle. He pointed to a flowing stream and said: 'Ye'll have to lep over that stream, first of all.' Turning to Omer he added, 'You might make it, but your mother will never make it.'

Meanwhile back in the mother abbey of Maredsous, expert advice was sought on how to invest the funds accumulating from Marmion's royalties. The advice was unanimous: invest in America. This was 1927. A year later the Wall Street Crash put paid to these investments. A telegram was sent to the settlers in the castle: 'No money. Come home.' But the pioneers had got a taste of their freedom and the magic of the landscape around them. They refused to go back.

The archbishop who issued the invitation in the first place, made it clear that he expected the monks to start a school in the monastery. In a letter dated 8th December, 1926 he wrote: 'With special pleasure, I give the community permission to establish a Benedictine house, at Glenstal, in the Archdiocese of Cashel. This permission extends to an arts and crafts school, which would be a great boon to ecclesiastical art in Ireland, and also to a higher school of general students, in which Irish students would hold a prominent place.'

The founding charter of this second school was pretty specific. Its purpose was to provide a suitable alternative for families who were sending their boys to England to be educated and to offer Catholic education of the highest quality to those perceived to be the future of this country. On the 19th January, 1928 at the inauguration of Glenstal Priory, Archbishop Harty gave the blessing and told the assembled guests that he had several personal reasons for rejoicing on that day: 'I see a religious community established in my native parish; I see the Irish flag displayed on these buildings; but above all, I rejoice to see the reintroduction of the famous Benedictine Order into Ireland.' He ended by reiterating his hope that the monks would establish a secondary boarding school which would have a great social influence on the future of the country.[52]

Nothing less than an invitation to found or to join a new aristocracy:

----

52   Mark Tierney, *Glenstal Abbey, An Historical Guide*, 5th Edition, 2009, pp. 43- 47.

We're the new aristocracy
We're the cream of society.
Though Dublin Castle has had its day
There's a brand new social set that is on its way!

Dad has a seat up in Leinster House
And he sits there just like a mouse
He always votes as he's told to do
If you we're in his place, that's what you'd do too!

We've a farm here in County Meath
Butter and Milk is the air we breathe
Money to be made in the land we ploughs
And you can make lot of friends with the help of cows

Oh, Yes you can walk with the elite
if your Dad's a judge or if he has a seat,
If you've lots of clothes, and look a wow,
You can make a lot of friends with the help of a cow!

Dad's a place in Fitzwilliam square
Young mamas bring their troubles there
They all think that he's very sweet
He don't know an awful lot
But he's so discreet

Architecture is Dad's domain
Church design is his source of gain
Though in his class he was near the end
He's got the best degree of all:
He's the bishop's friend.

Oh, Yes you can walk with the elite
if your Dad's a judge or if he has a seat,
If you've lots of clothes, and look a wow,
and you can make a lot of friends with the help of a cow![53]

I was sent to Glenstal Abbey School at the age of twelve in 1956. As I came to the end of my schooldays I wanted to find out where the God of Knockfierna had in mind for me to go. The monks at Glenstal were very sure that by joining them and becoming a monk I would have a failsafe way of finding out. I wasn't so sure. It seemed such a dull and dreary life. I decided to look for a sign and to lay a trap. I was doing the Leaving Certificate that year and I indicated the precise results which, if I got them exactly as proposed, would become a sign that the monastery was the way for me to go.

I went further, as my namesake the deceitful boy might have suggested. I made it as difficult as possible for these results to materialise. I had done five exams and was pretty sure that all these were in the bag as anticipated. I had two more to do and one of these would not be required for my matriculation. I had laid down as a requirement for the secret message from Knockfierna that an honours result in Geography would be mandatory. Geography was the last paper I had to sit. I decided to turn it into a farce, making a joke of the answers to all the questions posed. I remember well that one question was about the geological formation of mountains. I drew little comic faces in the margin with balloons coming from their mouths which said: 'If you want to make a mountain, go out and hire a weathering agent (ha, ha, ha!)'. I then went to great lengths

---

53 I heard this song performed in the Eblana Theatre in the early 1960s. It was part of a revue written by Fergus Lineahan. The text was lost without trace until it was sung for me again by Lelia Doolan and Rosaleen Linehan, wife of the lyricist, when we were together at Jennifer Johnston's ninetieth birthday celebration in the DLR Lexicon library in Dun Laoghaire. The Eblana theatre was situated in the basement of Bus Áras, Dublin's central bus station. A small theatre, seating 225-240 people, it was noted for being without wings and other common aspects of theatrical architecture, having been adapted from a short-lived newsreel cinema intended to entertain waiting bus passengers. It was open from 17th September, 1959 until 1995.

to explain that I had actually been present at the making of a mountain when I was six years old. In 1950 we had made a mountain in Ballingarry to celebrate the Holy Year. I explained that Knockfierna was only 964 feet high, which was thirteen feet short of being classified as a mountain. We had put a cement cross thirteen feet high on the top and turned the hill into a mountain overnight. It was the tractor from our farm that was used to bring the necessaries to the summit. To answer the question being posed in the exam therefore: all you needed to do the business was a few bags of cement and a Fordson Major. I left the examination hall with a mixture of guilt and glee. The *buachaill bréagach* had flung a stone and no stone had come back through *Poll na Bruíne*.

I could hardly believe my eyes, nor could I explain my shock to either parents or teachers, when the Leaving Cert results eventually came through. I had excelled in Geography. Either the person correcting my paper was from Knockfierna or they were so bored correcting predictable answer papers that my tomfoolery had tickled their fancy. My bluff, at any rate, had been called.

When I joined the monastery and made profession in 1963, my father took a sapling from the Turkish Oak beside the lake in front of Ballyneale and, with the help of Brother Finian Moran planted it beside the Chapel Lake here at Glenstal Abbey where it stands to this day to remind me of where I came from.

GLENWILLIAM

If you turned to the right on leaving Ballyneale House and drove a few miles towards Newcastlewest you would come upon Glenwilliam Castle. Not really a castle, it is a two-storey three-bay house with a curved bow in the centre, built by an unknown architect in 1797 for the Rev. William Massey. In the early 1830s George Massey added a castellated tower to the left of the original house, to the design, apparently, of James and George Richard Pain. They must also have designed the castellated outbuildings close to the house. A castle at any rate for all intents and purposes to the uninitiated outsider. Sometime later George lost the castle and the property on a gambling table in Wales where it was won by Edward Atkinson of Glenwilliam and Skea House, Enniskillen who then came to live in his newly acquired property at Ballingarry, Co. Limerick. He is on record in the 1870s as owning 2,655 acres there. He was father of John Atkinson, later created a Lord, who was Attorney General of Ireland in the 1890s and a Member of Parliament for North Derry. Edward married a second time and presumably because the son of his first marriage had been so successful, decided to leave his estates to the only son of this second marriage. Thomas Richard Durbin Atkinson inherited Glenwilliam Castle when his father died in 1876 and he himself was only a teenage boy. He came of age in 1884 and lived at Glenwilliam for the rest of his life.

Nan Coll, De Valera's mother, who was born in Bruree, came to work as a housemaid at Glenwilliam Castle. Tommy Atkinson, as he was known to his friends, developed a reputation as a randy landlord, whether this was based on established fact or later mythological weavings is not clear. Whoever may have been the cause, Nan Coll became pregnant while working at Glenwilliam Castle and had to go to America where she gave birth to a son in the Nursery and Child's Hospital, Manhattan, New York in 1882. The identity of De Valera's mother, Catherine Coll of Bruree, Limerick, never has been doubted. However the debate over the paternity of one of Ireland's greatest figures of the twentieth century remains open. Whatever the facts of the case, local history and imagination in Ballingarry, Co. Limerick records that De Valera was the son of Tommy Atkinson of Glenwilliam Castle.

Scholarly historians trying to establish evidence for this conjecture claim that his fees at Blackrock College, where he went to school, were subsidised by Atkinson and his arrival on the political scene in the East-Clare by-election was sponsored by the same source. However, the *pièce de résistance* in this search for proof is the suggestion that De Valera's reprieve from execution after the 1916 rising which many attributed to his American citizenship, was also influenced by Tommy Atkinson, whose half-brother had become a significant figure in the Irish legal world of that time.

Tommy Atkinson died in 1935 and Glenwilliam Castle became the property of his only surviving daughter Sibyl. She had married on St Patrick's Day, 1919 Colonel John Penry Garnons Worlledge. They had two daughters, Wendy and Annabel. Her husband John died in 1957, leaving Sibyl a widow in Glenwilliam Castle.

Sybil had a physical as well as a verbal twitch. She pronounced 'r' as 'w' and so everyone was 'tewwiffic' and everything was 'gwand'. At the same time one corner of her mouth would jerk sideways towards her ear, giving the impression of an insect-eating plant waiting to become carnivorous.

Although she didn't ride herself, she was a staunch promoter of the Limerick Hunt. Glenwilliam Castle was one of the privileged sites where a Lawn Meet would be held on a rotating basis. Being also a meticulous upholder of Divine Law, her hospitality was extended to all-comers with one provision: no divorcees were allowed inside her house. This meant that a very tiny minority would gather in her hall to 'dwink shewwy' while the rambunctious mob of Limerick Hunters drank their uproarious stirrup cup outside, imitating Sibyl and dwinking her champagne.

Sibyl advertised the castle for sale in 1946. When a buyer came forward she got cold feet and refused to complete the sale. This led to legal action but she won her case and remained impecuniously in her castle. Sibyl was a formidable dowager especially to those of us who were children in the region.

Whatever about the scholars and begrudgers, Sibyl Worlledge had no doubt whatsoever that Eamon De Valera was her 'half-brother'. Whenever he appeared within range of her stomping ground, she would get into her car and dwive to wherever he was to appear. She would throw herself upon him as a long-lost relative and inform the gaping multitudes that he was her half-brother. The news appalled both Dev and his supporters. Neighbours would try to flatter Sibyl and promote her cause by saying that she looked the spitting image of Dev. However much this might validate her contention or improve her prospects in the new republic, it was a doubtful compliment to her own feminine good looks.

As children we would be invited to visit her and climb the tower of Glenwilliam Castle. Such visits were ghoulish affairs like the visits of Pip to Miss Havisham in *Great Expectations*, where he was commandeered to 'play' as a way of cheering her up. When she heard that I was joining a monastery she insisted on an interview. I entered her gloomy room where she sat on an armchair surrounded by all her underclothes that were hanging after washing on various hooks and hangers around her chair in front of the only stove that kept her warm in the enormous house. I sat in front of her and without talking she fished a garment from the stove with her stick and waved it in front of my nose. 'Ever seen one of these,' she asked, the corner of her mouth sliding westward in a grin that took it way beyond her jaw. The piece of dangling cloth looked like a miniature hammock on a string. 'It's a bwazier,' she exclaimed, as if exhibiting some wild animal she had shot. 'Until you've taken off one or two of these, you have no business going into that prison-house. You listen to me.' I thanked her for her concern and fled from the castle.

VI

Life as a Limerick

How to break down two worlds and bring them together again? Imagination, education, poetry. There had always been poetry in this part of the world.

Limerick must be one of the few places that has a genre of poetry named after it, or having the same name as it. Whether that is because the name Limerick, coming from 'lom' meaning 'bare' and 'eanach' meaning 'swamp' or 'lom an eich' a place eaten bare by horses, the etymology is never very flattering.[54]

No one is claiming that the Limerick was invented or first used here. People quote Aristophanes, the fourth century BCE Greek comic poet; others will say it was brought back from France as barrack-room ballads by veterans of the Irish Brigade. Who knows?

The word limerick as a kind of poem did not officially enter the English language until 1989, according to the Oxford English Dictionary, whose founder Sir James Murray defined it, quite unfairly, as an indecent nonsense verse.

The limerick is furtive and mean;
You must keep him in close quarantine
Or he sneaks to the slums
And promptly becomes
Disorderly, drunk and obscene.

....

54   Matthew Potter, *The Curious Story of the Limerick*, Limerick, LWC, 2017.

Some limericks are indeed so, but as the American poet Donald Marquis says:

> It needn't have ribaldry's taint
> Or strive to make anyone faint.
> There's a type that's demure
> And perfectly pure,
> Though it helps quite a lot
> if it ain't.

What we do know is that the form was used in Irish by the eighteenth century Maigue poets, and that it eventually got its name from the place where it has been most used and is most useful.

So what exactly is it?

The Limerick as a poem has five lines. The first two rhyme with each other and with the last line. Lines three and four are an independently rhyming couplet with six syllables in each line. The triplet of lines one, two and five comprise nine syllables in each line. And if all that is too complicated, here's how it goes in practice:

> There was a young fellah from Sydney,
> Who drank till it ruined his kidney
> He drank and he drank
> While it shrivelled and shrank
> But he did have fun doing it, didn't he.

In the 1980s the *Irish Times* set an annual Limerick competition which always attracted a huge response. In April 1986, the winner of the 'Limericks Galore' competition no. 883 was James Evans from Dublin. His winning entry could have been written specifically for our purposes:

There was an old maid from Macroom
Who kept a pet horse in her room,
Asked why, she replied:
If I can't be a bride
Then the least I can be is a groom.

Poetry is the only language that can reach down to the deepest roots of things displaying their infrastructure. As you might cry out in pain when you stub your toe, poetry issues from a similar gutland. The shorter the poem, the sharper the shout. 'What you start from is nothing so definite as an emotion, in any ordinary sense; it is still more certainly not an idea; it is - to adapt two lines of Beddoes to a different meaning – 'a bodiless childful of life in the gloom/ Crying with frog voice, "what shall I be?" The poet is sometimes oppressed by a burden which must be brought to birth in order to obtain relief. Or, the poet is haunted by a demon which in its first manifestation has no face, no name, nothing; and the words, the poem, are a kind of exorcism of this demon.'[55] So, that explains why Limerick is a good place for such poems.

We have been too rational in the past. We have imagined that we could examine the world we live in as if we were able to survey it from an omni-directional swivel tower in our heads, looking down and around us. The truth of our situation is not like that. In fact, we are buried right up to our foreheads in the earthy mud we are trying to examine. And the language squeezed out of our larynxes from the depths of our guts, is the only one which can encompass the embodied situation we are in from the moment we are born to the last gasp we utter from our earth. This long-winded death-rattle is the pulsating oxygen of poetry. It is a way in which human consciousness can reach beyond and below the normal modality of thinking.

Each one of us is required to understand why we are alive at this moment on this planet where we were stranded without our consent. No

....

55   T.S. Eliot, *The Three Voices of Poetry*, Cambridge University Press, 1953, p 4.

one can do this work for us, we are obliged to undertake it for ourselves, first person singular, present tense. Poetry provides a language for such existential expression. Poets are those who can handle language in ways that allow it to express the otherwise inexpressible. We are lucky if there are a handful of such poets in each generation, and if we can understand what they are trying to say.

W.B. Yeats says somewhat arrogantly and imperiously: 'It is not the business of the poets to make themselves understood; it is the business of the people to understand them.' He was supercilious but he was right. Poets when they are doing their job are speaking the truth and it is up to us, if we want to be their contemporaries, to understand what they are saying, sometimes obliquely through these poems. We need interpreters: those who can tell us clearly what the poets are saying to us confusedly.

The Maigue Poets: Filí ma Máighe

The River Maigue, which means 'river of the plain' rises in north county Cork and is almost forty miles long, before it flows into the Atlantic from the Shannon estuary. On its way it is joined by the small river Glen and the larger river Loobah in South County Limerick, when it reaches Bruree. From here it is augmented by the river Morning Star before flowing through Croom, which takes its name from the 'bend in the river,' and on to Adare (the ford of the oak). The school of poets called after the river survived in Croom up to the 1770s and was known for its use of the five line Limerick. As a group they shared views in common on a wide variety of subjects, including religion, nationality, poetry and the Irish language. They tried to promote and preserve the age-old culture of the Gael which they saw being superseded by the new, alien culture of the Gall.

The two recognised founders of the Maigue Poets in Croom were Sean Ó Tuama and his friend Andrias MacRaith, both of whom grew up in Kilmallock. O'Tuama went on to become a publican. Meetings of the poets took place in his pub in Croom and later in Limerick City. He was a generous patron and many of the bards took advantage of his generosity, which his wife regarded as reckless prodigality precipitating their eventual financial ruin. Andrias, who called himself the Merry Pedlar, often drank too much and offended with his biting tongue. Most of what I know about him comes from Mannix Joyce who wrote extensively about Limerick for nearly fifty years using the pseudonym *An Mangaire Súgach*, the Merry Peddlar, which he borrowed from Andrias.

Because of the not-always model life that Andrias led, he got into trouble with the clergy from time to time. The climax came in 1738, when both the Protestant minister and the parish priest of Croom, banished him from the parish. Broken-hearted, he removed to Ballyneety only to find that his reputation had gone before him and the people there would hardly speak to him. It was from this exile that he addressed to Seán Ó Tuama his most famous poem *Slán le Máigh*, the first line of which, *Ó Scoladh mé chun uignes* (since I was sent away to loneliness) almost sums up his life.

Ó Tuama seems to have established himself as the recognised bard of the area. He would be called upon to write a poem on various topics and on occasions which called for poetic celebration or excoriation. One such concerned a Dominican priest with my own name, Hederman, who had done the unspeakable of becoming a Protestant minister. I find my relative described in a footnote as 'an old, half-crazed Irish friar named Thomas Hederman who, at different stages of a long career, had been a novice in Rome, a lector at Louvain, an apostate, a Protestant minister in Limerick, and a Dominican missionary in the French West Indies'.[56]

O frogspawn of Dominic's preachers
My mind has gown dizzy with tears
At the thought of your act which disfeatures
The order you share with your peers

[56] Una Nic Einrí and Milo Spillane, *Seán O Tuama, ó Chromadh an tSubhachais*, Dublin, Coiscéim, 2012 p. 224.

An order vowed holy to Mary
That no other women despoil
This humpbacked obscene dromedary
Has flaunted! It makes my blood boil.

His treacherous back may be laden
With ill-gotten treasures galore
He has wilfully left the fair maiden
To set up his tent with a whore

To change from a priest to a parson
an action unworthy of note
If guilty of murder or arson
At least he could hang by the throat

Think not for one second true pastors
What such dereliction might spell
This son of yours, truly a bastard
is going directly to hell

Forget the disgrace that befalls you
Your order can rally its pride
His apostasy justly appals you
Like Esau he's let down the side

Each family must take its chances
What matter the question he begs
He fell from the noblest of branches
By choice he consorts with the dregs

Envoi

Lock him up and throw the key
Over the wall and into the night
He betrayed his God, Blest Trinity
Hederman, crock full of shite.[57]

Although Ó Tuama and MacCraith were friends and fellow champions of the Maigue poets, they fell out and wrote bitter satires castigating each other in rhyme. Below are believed to be the first 'Limericks' written at the time.

Ó Tuama wrote:

I sell the best Brandy and Sherry
to make all my customers merry.
But at times their finances
run short as it chances.
And then I feel very sad, very.

MacCraith, who apparently felt himself compromised by the above, replied:

Ó Tuama, you boast yourself handy,
at selling good ale and bright Brandy,
But the fact is your liquor
makes everyone sicker
I tell you this I, your friend Andy.

A more recent battle of the Limericks took place in the pages of the *Limerick Leader* between Richard Harris, the famous actor from Limerick city and the playwright John B. Keane from Listowel. John B. had written a famous

....

57   This is quite a famous satire written in eighteenth century Irish using the 'aoar' format. The accentual metres popular at the time feature complex systems of internal rhymes difficult to convey in translation. I am indebted to Edel Bhreathnach for supplying me with her translation which allowed me to forge this contemporary equivalent, for which Edel is in no way to be blamed or held responsible.

play in 1965 called *The Field* which he based on an actual and unfortunate occurrence at Reamore, Co. Kerry in 1959 where a bachelor farmer, Moss Moore, had died in suspicious circumstances never satisfactorily resolved. His neighbour, Dan Foley, was suspected but never proven to be the murderer. Local people decided that Dan had done the deed and made his life hell until he too eventually died. John B. Keane was inspired to write his play on the basis of this incident although he always claimed that his work was fiction and not history. The main character, The Bull McCabe, was a protagonist of epic proportions and 'lust for land' was the motivation for his tragic story.

The play was staged at the Abbey with Ray McAnally in the leading role. This was rural Ireland in the raw. Audiences attuned to the *The Quiet Man* of John Ford's earlier film were shocked and horrified. In 1991 Jim Sheridan scripted and directed a Hollywood movie based on the play. Ray McAnally was again supposed to play the main part in the film but his untimely death in 1989 made it necessary to find an alternative. Richard Harris was chosen. His performance was well received and he was nominated both for an Oscar and a Golden Globe. There was one protestor. John B. Keane was not impressed. He and Harris argued the toss in a series of letters in the early 1990s to the *Limerick Leader*.

RH:

A writer whose plays might be seen
In a shed down some country boreen
Has the nerve to suggest
That his works at their best
should appear on a Hollywood screen

And that's where Dick Harris steps in
They need his provocative grin
Without a great actor
Aboard your old tractor
You can throw J.B. Keane in the bin

JB:

When *The Field* was first staged in the full
One person was dyed-in-the wool
The great Ray McAnally
Let's not shilly-shally
Was born for the part of 'The Bull.'

When they gave Richard Harris the part
He adopted his own arty-fart
He ruined my play
With the ham-fisted way
He murdered the Bull from the start.

It was Hamlet on steroids no doubt
Every line interchanged for a shout
He was purely delighted
He thought he'd be knighted
Not a clue what the play was about

They died in two thousand and two
That ended the hullaballoo
They both have a statue
That's staring straight at you
As if to say: 'Over to you!

They began with no stone left unthrown
They ended like Darby and Joan
Before they departed
As if nothing had started
They drank a pint over the phone

In an attempt to revive The Maigue poetry tradition, celebrities were invited from all over the world to read those poems they had been hiding in their desks, ashamed to face the limelight. On one occasion, I remember when I was a youth, they invited Idi Amin to come and read his poetry. This was before he had established his reputation as a genocidal monster and was known only as an entertaining showman who also wrote poems. It was said that the last medal of the twenty-four that were clustered across his large expanse of chest was presented to him by the Catholic Boy Scouts of Ireland. A telegram came from Uganda to the organisers asking the measurements of the airport in Croom to establish whether the poet would be able to land his private jet there minutes before he gave his poetry reading. He also wanted to know the exact amount of appearance money he might expect which was to be paid in American dollars. The invitation was *a cuir ar an mhéar fháda*, put on the long finger.

VII

The Black and Amber

Whatever about intermarriage between Protestants and Catholics, the biggest sensation had yet to come. My Aunt Ethel lived in Croom in a house partly designed by herself called Glenwood. Because of her own insistent help with the architecture, all sorts of exciting corners and corridors revealed themselves like ancient priestholes where the drawing-room never quite made it to the dining room and left a corridor in between, which set off on its own going nowhere in particular at a tangent.

There was one tennis court out front. The first Open championships in Ireland, she would have you know, took place in August 1877, the same year as the first All-England championships of Wimbledon. The event was not held in Dublin but at the Limerick Lawn Tennis Club, nostalgically referred to as the 'County' Limerick Lawn, putting Limerick in a premier position on the tennis map predating Fitzwilliam Lawn Tennis Club by two years. Aunt Ethel would throw parties for 200 people all dressed in white to play tennis on this one court. Knowledge of or expertise in the game were not required. Four people who were especially invited could look after that performance on the red brick hardcourt which doubled with an herbaceous border where most of the one tube of tennis balls got lost. What was required was that only 'the right sort of people' should turn up. Bishops of both denominations were always invited although not required to wear fancy dress. On one occasion she is said to have invited guests, forgotten all about them and returned to her house late in the evening to find endless numbers dressed in white wandering aimlessly around outside.

Her husband, who had been the local doctor, died leaving her a widow with four children. She set herself up as a painter of sorts specialising in horses. Her masterpiece was a three-legged horse which won much critical acclaim. The search for the fourth leg was subject of many social occasions and eventually turned itself into a party game.

Aunt Ethel would shop in Limerick and park her car in the middle of the road while she would dash into Todds or Spaights for whatever item she required. People from the county went to certain shops: Nestor's for cartridges and sports supplies. Tom Nestor would engage his clients in long discussion about fly fishing and where the salmon might rise. Only Mr Wogan could look after you personally in Leverett and Frye at the top of O'Connell Street. He might even take your parcel for you out to the car. Terry Wogan was nowhere to be seen and only later became the person one might wish to speak to.

All this was possible until the dreaded arrival of traffic wardens who would unreasonably curtail your parking rights and insert a vulgar looking ticket in the windscreen wiper of your car, parked at an angle in the middle of the road. Aunt Ethel caught one such female warden *flagrante delicto* as she was depositing her junk mail on the windscreen. Appealing to Mr Wogan, who was following her, a reluctant mule from Leverett and Frye, she declared her credentials as a grieving widow. And to boot it was Christmas time. 'Ah, now,' she cooed at the traffic lady, 'that's not a very nice present to be leaving on my windscreen in the season of goodwill.' Getting no encouragement or confirmation from Mr Wogan, she had to turn on the agony all by herself.

'My husband died at Christmastime of the year,' she said. (She did not mention how many years ago).

'I just lost my mother,' snapped the unyielding traffic warden.

'Oh you poor thing,' warbled Aunt Ethel, 'I know how you feel, I know what it is to lose a dear one ...'

'Nonsense,' cried the traffic warden, securing the parking ticket even more viciously to the windscreen, 'You only lost a husband. You can get a husband any day but you can never get back your mother.'

Living contemporaneously at Springfort in Patrickswell, five miles down the road was a Protestant family called Kennedy. Fred had been a major in Probyn's Horse, a cavalry regiment in the Indian Army from 1938 to 1947. Born in Ireland he had been sent to school in England and went to university at Cambridge. His wife, whom everyone called 'Bin,' had owned a farm in Dorset, but because Fred had always wanted to return to Ireland and specifically to County Limerick, they came here after the war. They had two daughters, Amber and Susan. All four were regular riders at the hunt. Amber was very fair and strikingly beautiful, and as Percy French would say: 'Every man had got the finest plan you ever see now.'

One day Aunt Ethel climbed into her car and drove all the way to our house to tell my mother the staggering news that Amber Kennedy was going to marry 'a pure black'. Whatever about inter-marriage between Protestants and Catholics, this was an unheard of combination in County Limerick.

Rodger was from New Kensington in Pennsylvania. Amber and he got married in a civil ceremony at City Hall in New York, with one friend who was moving to California that day and another witness pulled from out of the queue. Tony Tarry said it would be one thing if Rodger had been to Eton or Harrow, or even Oxford or Cambridge, "One would know where he came from." But an American! "For all we know, he could be descended from slaves!"

Amber's mother and father were opposed to the marriage. Her father said there was no moral or ethical argument against it but he could not accept it. However, he agreed that she could not be forced to think as her parents thought. He himself had been cut off from his inheritance because his mother disapproved of his marrying Bin, whose father was a Catholic and whose mother was Jewish. Fred died of a heart-attack before Amber and Rodger actually got married, which caused a friend of her family from Limerick to tell Amber that she had been responsible for killing her father. One of the last things Fred Kennedy asked, as his aorta was bursting, was 'Will I be able to hunt again?'

The only person from Limerick who wrote to Amber to encourage her was Bill Harrington's youngest daughter Sarah Stanhope, who advised her to ignore what people were saying and go for it with Rodger. Sarah was herself in trouble because the man she was hoping to marry was Bobby Barry from Bruff. When Amber showed her letter to Rodger he asked 'Is Bobby black?' Amber told him that it was far worse than that, Bobby was a Catholic.

A people set apart

Were we more racist and bigoted than others on the planet at the time? We were certainly more isolated, more sequestered as an island. In 2002 David Trimble, leader of the Ulster Unionist Party and first minister in Northern Ireland, presumably in an attempt to advance the so-called Peace Process and improve cross-border relations between the two parts of our Christian country, described the Republic of Ireland as 'monoethnic, monocultural, pathetic and sectarian'. This sounded and was meant to sound, insulting. But, I ask myself, is it not possible that every person born on this planet is by nature 'monoethnic, monocultural, pathetic and sectarian'. Is this not the way we are constituted? If we were not, might we ever have survived as a species? We are selfish, short-sighted and anti-social by definition, otherwise we might have been eliminated by other species competing for hegemony. Whatever our hopes about progress in terms of history and civilisation, should we not recognise, as Herbert Butterfield suggests, that each one of us is born 'equidistant from barbarity'?

When I had the privilege of living in Africa for a number of years, I was greatly relieved to find that, taken to remote places in Nigeria where so-called 'white' people had never been seen in the flesh, little children would run away from me screaming in terror. They had to be taken up by their mothers to reassure them as they touched my face that I was not a monster but a human being just like themselves. It seems that we are afraid of whatever is unfamiliar and only regular experience of variety and difference develops our capacity for empathy and tolerance.

Nigeria was the showpiece of Ireland's 'religious empire'. The greatest concentration of Irish missionaries in the world was to be found there. Of the country's 850 Catholic priests, more than 500 were Irish. The country had become a formally independent federation on 1ˢᵗ October, 1960. The modern state originated from British Colonial Rule beginning in the nineteenth century, and took its present territorial shape with the merging of the Southern Nigeria Protectorate and the northern Nigeria Protectorate in 1914, overseen by Lord Frederick Lugard. 'The fact remains,' says Chinua Achebe, 'that Nigeria was created by the British, for their own ends.' The British set up administrative and legal structures while practicing indirect rule through traditional chiefdoms. Numerous ancient African civilisations settled in the region that is known today as Nigeria. This artificially created country houses over 250 diverse and often antagonistic tribal groups. These were forced into national identity when granted independence by Britain in 1960. The country is still very much a tribal society where local alliances count for more than national attachments.

Both Nigeria and Ireland, as countries colonised by England, became English speaking. Of course there are those who still deplore this eventuality and would try to persuade us to make Irish once more our *lingua franca*. There is another point of view expressed here by Bill Bryson among others: 'All the evidence suggests that minority languages shrink or thrive at their own ineluctable rate. It seems not to matter greatly whether governments suppress them brutally or support them lavishly. Despite all the encouragement and subsidisation given to Gaelic in Ireland, it is spoken by twice as many people in Scotland, where there has been negligible government assistance.' This view is confirmed in the recent Cambridge History of Ireland which states: 'Notwithstanding many inducements, financial resources and patriotic exhortations, the decline of Irish has continued.'[58] Although the imposition of English came about through colonial oppression, the results offer distinct advantages again enumerated by Bill Bryson:

....

[58] Thomas Bartlett, *The Cambridge History of Ireland*, Volume IV, *1880 to the Present*, Cambridge University Press, 2018, p. xxxiii.

We naturally lament the decline of these languages, but it is not an altogether undiluted tragedy. Consider the loss to English literature if Joyce, Shaw, Swift, Yeats, Wilde, Synge ... and Ireland's other literary geniuses had written in what is inescapably a fringe language ... No country has given the world more incomparable literature per head of population than Ireland, and for that reason alone we might be excused a small, selfish celebration that English was the language of her greatest writers.[59]

The same is probably even more true for Nigeria, where over 525 native languages are spoken. Their official language is now English, which not only allows for communication with the rest of the world in what has become ever-increasingly a universal language, but it also allows Nigerians to communicate with each other.

As in Ireland, English has been adopted culturally and artistically in a way that has enriched world literature. English is no longer the prerogative or the possession of any one people, even if it emerged from one particular place. Other countries and other peoples have appropriated it in ways that splice it into their own indigenous cultures and vocabularies to enrich it and make it unrecognisable when compared with what it was before it passed through such transformation.

Probably the earliest Nigerian artist who broke through to recognised international literary achievement was Gabrial Okara (1921–2019). Adrian Roscoe sees in Okara 'something of the Celtic colour of soul, with its sensitivity and large resources of sadness, yet without the Celtic sense of humour'.[60] However, it is Chinua Achebe (1930–2013) who creates an artistic link between the Irish and Nigerian experience both of history and of literature. *Things Fall Apart,* his début novel (1958) takes its title from 'The Second Coming' of W.B. Yeats. Achebe chronicles pre-colonial life in the south-eastern part of Nigeria and describes the arrival

59   Bill Bryson, *Mother Tongue, The English Language,* Penguin Books, London, 1991, pp. 36-37.
60   Adrian Roscoe, *Mother is Gold,* Cambridge University Press, 1971, p. 28.

of Europeans in the late nineteenth century. His second novel *No Longer at Ease* tells of Obi Okonkwo, from the Igbo tribe, who leaves his village for an education in Britain. He returns home to a job in the Nigerian colonial civil service. Torn between African culture and Western lifestyle, he ends up taking a bribe.

Achebe describes the clash between European and traditional cultures which has become entrenched during the long period of colonial rule. The book's title comes from the closing lines of T.S. Eliot's 'Journey of the Magi':

> We returned to our places, these Kingdoms,
> But no longer at ease here,
> With an alien people clutching their gods.
> I should be glad of another death.

Arrow of God (1964) the third novel of the trilogy, introduces Ezeulu chief priest of the God Ulu who is worshipped by the six villages of Umuaro. Ezeulu and Umuaro are fighting against the nearby village Okperi. The conflict is resolved when T. K. Winterbottom, the British colonial overseer, intervenes. After the conflict, a Christian missionary, John Goodcountry arrives in Umuaro. He tells the villagers tales of Nigerians in the Niger Delta who have abandoned their religion in favour of Christianity. Many of the villagers have already lost their faith in Ezeulu. One of Ezeulu's sons, Obika, dies during a traditional ceremony, which the villagers interpret as a sign that Ulu has taken sides with them against his priest. For this apparent judgement against Ezeulu and because of the immunity promised by the Christian God, many embrace Christianity. It is easy to understand how many Irish interpreters are ready to identify with such a narrative.

The book which opened my eyes and described the link between Ireland and Africa was *Myth, Literature and the African World*, especially the essay in the appendix called 'The Fourth Stage'.[61] Wole Soyinka won the Nobel Prize for Literature in 1986, the first time such a prize had been awarded to an African writer from the 'new literatures' in English emerging from former British colonies on that continent. Soyinka's mother tongue is Yoruba and even though he has translated from Yoruba into English, most of his creative work has been in English. Theatre is Soyinka's most powerful medium. He bases many of his plays on ancient traditional rites and ceremonies taken from Yoruba culture. Theatre becomes the x-ray machine that allows us to observe the bone structure of the world as this culture sees it. Every item on the stage makes up, at one level, a recognisable geographical location, but, when loosened up and disentangled by music and dance, they become a deeper-laid contour map of another country. His plays open passageways to a world other than the one inhabited by most people on a daily basis. Ant-hills in Nigeria, like fairy forts in Ireland, are openings into an alternative space inhabited by the dead, by the ancestors. Some of these plays are attempts to make present the spatio-temporal structure of this invisible world, contiguous to our own.

In *Dance of the Forests*, the play performed as part of Nigerian Independence celebrations in October 1960, and in *The Swamp Dwellers*, the forest and the swamp on stage represent that 'other' world, out of which can come those capable of making the 'transition' to our world'. The scene is a hut on stilts, built on one of the semi-firm islands which mirror the kind of world we inhabit.

Biafra: Ireland's black baby

The so-called Nigerian Civil War (also known as the Biafran War) was fought between the Nigerian government and the secessionist state of Biafra from 6th July, 1967 to 15th January, 1970. Biafra represented

---

61 Wole Soyinka, *Myth, Literature and the African World*, Cambridge University Press, 1976, Canto Edition, 1990. This book was given to me by Sister Jo O'Donovan as I left for Nigeria in 1992.

nationalist aspirations of the Igbo people whose leadership felt they could no longer coexist with the Northern-dominated federal government. The conflict resulted from political, economic, ethnic, cultural and religious tensions which preceded Britain's formal decolonisation of Nigeria.

Emeka Odumegwu-Ojukwu (1933-2011) was certainly a charismatic figure. His father was a business tycoon, Nigeria's first billionaire, who was awarded an OBE and a title from the Queen of England. He was known as Sir Louis Phillip Odumegwu Ojukwu, OBE. Emeka, his son, was educated in England and had a degree from Oxford. He was one of the first and few university graduates to receive an army commission. At that time, the Nigerian Military Forces had 250 officers and only 15 were Nigerian. On the 30th May, 1967, as a result of many months of failed negotiations, Colonel Odumegwu-Ojukwu declared Eastern Nigeria a sovereign state to be known as Biafra. On 6th July 1967, General Yakubu ('Jack') Gowon declared war on Biafra.

In Ojukwu's view: 'Nigeria is the one true giant of Africa. Her peoples constitute nearly one half of the black people of the continent and two in five of all black people in the world. The resources concentrated within her borders would be the envy of most countries in Europe and the Americas, her landmass is huge, her climate largely benign. All this should have made her not only the most powerful country in the black world, but among the dozen most powerful nations on the globe.'

Ojukwu communicated these views to the then BBC correspondent covering the war, Frederick Forsythe, who was so impressed by the Biafran leader that he wrote his biography.[62] Forsythe began as a BBC correspondent but was so aware of their prejudice against Biafra that he left his job and returned to Nigeria to report and support the Biafran cause. His biography of Emeka paints an impressive picture of the Nigerian leader but it has been faulted as being partisan and uncritical. He was certainly exaggeratedly respectful of Ojukwu.

....

62   Frederick Forsythe, *Emeka*, Spectrum Books, Ibaden, Nigeria, 1982. Cf. also Emeka Odumegwu-Ojukwu, *Because I am involved*, Ibaden, Nigeria, 1989.

Emeka's analysis of Nigerian failure to measure up to its potential includes bad government: 'Without organisation a society is destined to seize up, choke and eventually die. A state where the services do not function, where the citizenry is not disciplined, where crime at every level runs unchecked, where leaders are not accountable to the led, and where justice is available to the highest bidder - such a state cannot inspire in others outside that confidence needed for leadership abroad.'

Driving around Abuja I found an equivalent to my hill of truth in Zuma Rock, a large natural monolith along the main road to Kaduna, ten feet lower than Knockfierna. Emeka had interesting observations in this regard. He saw himself as a black man inheriting a religion of a kind other than mine.

Being black, according to Emeka, means having a certain concept of life, which, as for the Celts, involves a closeness to nature. However, this is accompanied by a great fear of the supernatural. He tried, over the years, 'to find at what point the road of evolution of the black man moved away from that taken by the white'. He sees that very turning-point to be in our relation to God. 'The fact is, the black man's God is a God of retribution; awesome, unapproachable and merciless. The white man's God is a God of love, mercy and forgiveness.'

He gives as an example the very situation I am describing in this book. Far from having the curious and consoling experience of God's presence on Knockfierna, the Nigerian faced with an equivalent mountain such as Zuma Rock, 'turns his back on this terrifying monster, seeks out a calf from his miserable herd and begins the regular sacrifice to the god of the mountain'. The mountain may very well become sacred in both cases, as Knockfierna is for me, but this would make it in Africa, according to Emeka, fearsome and impenetrable. Whereas I could be fascinated and drawn to the spectacle of the mountain, anxious to climb it, and from its summit to survey the surrounding landscape, Emeka, as a black man, in his understanding of our corresponding situations, would consider himself unworthy of God, and unwilling to interfere or tamper with Creation.

'The white man,' says Emeka, 'considering himself a favourite of God, has, through the ages continually questioned Creation, and never hesitated to bend it to his will and his advantage.' Such attitudes have led to the huge technological gap between peoples, the domination of the world by the white, and the moral enslavement of the black person's mind.

> For me, Black means in a word 'disadvantaged'. The moral and emotional fabric of Western Civilisation is based on the concept that Black and inferior are synonymous ... Today I think we have come to realise that this bar to our development can and must be overcome. But to overcome it we must, as a race, make fundamental changes in our attitudes, realising that the greater enemy is within ourselves, and that plots and conspiracies against us, if they exist, are but secondary obstacles.'[63]

Although very few countries recognised the right of Biafra to secede - the annual conference of the Organisation for African Unity that September of 1967 called for an end to hostilities, asked the rebels to make peace with the federal authorities and rejected support for secession by 33 votes to 4 - and although the Irish Minister for Foreign Affairs, Frank Aiken rejected the argument of self-determination for the Igbos - arguing that 'to allow a single tribe to hive off on its own' would set a precedent for the other two hundred to demand autonomy[64] - there can be no doubt that the sympathies of the Irish people as a whole were firmly with Biafra. Whatever the historical facts, whatever the ins and outs, the rights and wrongs, and there were terrible sufferings inflicted, it is also true that we in Ireland took possession of this conflict and projected onto it archetypal shapes from our own historical

----

63 Frederick Forsythe, *Emeka*, Spectrum Books, Ibaden, Nigeria, 1982. Cf. also Emeka Odumegwu-Ojukwu, *Because I am involved*, Ibaden, Nigeria, 1989. In the 2003 edition, pp. 129-131.

64 Enda Staunton, 'The case of Biafra: Ireland and the Nigerian civil war,' *Irish Historical Studies*, Vol. 31, Issue 124, November 1999, pp. 513-534.

situation. We told our own story about the Nigerian conflict. Biafra was around the same size as Ireland.[65] The war had major repercussions for Irish missionary orders, many of whose members were expelled by the Nigerian authorities for allegedly having collaborated and/or encouraged the rebel Igbos. Ireland as a whole began to identify with the Igbos and project onto the Biafran war fantasies which mirrored our own fight for freedom from the British.

Kate O'Brien, writing in *The Irish Times*, summed up a general sense of devastation among the Irish people regarding the failure of the Biafran state. She wrote, 'We are all, everywhere, overclouded now by Nigeria, by dead Biafra ... we are for once together in real and baffled distress - for a country we have never set foot in, and a people we do not know. ... We can be said to be in a condition of humiliated woe, and helpless anger.'

There can be no doubt that once war was declared, it was an horrific human tragedy. Apart from the casualties caused by air-raids and warfare, after two-and-a-half years of war, almost two million Biafran civilians (three-quarters of them children) died from starvation caused by the total blockade of the region by the Nigerian government. So great was the suffering and so shocking the devastation caused by this gruesome struggle which was publicised worldwide by the media, that *Médecins Sans Frontières* was founded in response to this much publicised catastrophe. No one in the world could fail to be moved by the shocking pictures of the casualties from this cruel subjugation of the people of Biafra. However, it is one thing to deplore the atrocities of warfare, it is quite another to take sides in terms of the reasons and the initiation of the war in the first place and also of its outcomes.

The many texts and documents associated with Irish engagement in the war and famine in Biafra raise a number of questions regarding

---

65 Biafra has terrestrial borders shared with Nigeria to the north and west, and with Cameroon to the east. Its coast is on the Gulf of Guinea in the south bordering the South Atlantic Ocean. Biafra's land mass covers 29,848 square miles (77,310 km²), whereas Ireland's is 32,599 square miles (84,421 km²).

Irish identity and affinities. Although the official story of Irish state engagement with the war—the diplomatic efforts to protect Irish citizens in Nigeria and to establish the truth in the face of propaganda—may be discovered in the National Archives, the story of the public's experience of the war is largely to be found in the news media.

The Irish government maintained diplomatic relations with Nigeria throughout the war, and refused to grant official recognition to the state of Biafra. Because of the strong missionary connections and extensive Irish fundraising initiatives of the time, a mention of Biafra often evokes the popular 'memory' that Ireland supported Biafra in the conflict. The causes of the war and the events that motivated the Biafran declaration of independence are less well understood or remembered than is the subsequent famine and the terrible images of starvation which came to be associated with the name 'Biafra'.

Of course, the intense Irish relationship with the short-lived Republic of Biafra (it ceased to exist in January 1970) had its origins in a number of factors and the story, though largely forgotten today, provides an example of the instrumentality of the media in forming public opinion. The most important factors that contributed to an Irish sense of closeness to Biafra, and which helps to explain how local structures provided access to the events as well as a framework that enabled the transformation of the distant conflict into a local concern, was Ireland's missionary history in Africa.[66]

The Irish missionary relationship with Eastern Nigeria had begun in 1902 when Joseph Shanahan, a priest of the Holy Ghost Order, first arrived in Nigeria. In appearance he was an impressive figure, tall and athletic, and accounts of his work in Africa frequently compared him to St Patrick, who had converted the pagan Irish.

....
66   Fiona Bateman "Ireland and the Nigeria-Biafra War: Local Connections to a Distant Conflict", *New Hibernia Review / Iris Éireannach Nua*, vol. 16, no. 1, 2012, pp. 48–67. *JSTOR*, www.jstor.org/stable/23266639. Accessed 23rd January, 2021.

It was the missionary network on the ground in Biafra which supplied much of the first-hand information and the photographs of the horrors being perpetrated. Here, for instance, is Fr Denis Kennedy describing his attempt to bring French TV crews to Owerri after its recapture by the Biafran troops, in one of the biggest battles of the war. They had come into the country to record the event and prove to the world that the town had been retaken and Nigeria had suffered a significant setback:

> The scene that greeted us as we entered the town was horrific. Along the roadside lay skeletons clad in nothing but army boots, with discs around their necks. The vultures had eaten everything else, both flesh and clothing. The TV crew filmed furiously. The streets were strewn with shell casings, cartridges, rubble and corpses. Finally, we came to enormous mounds of munitions and trucks which had been destroyed by the Nigerians before they fled the town lest they fall into Biafran hands.[67]

This was a propaganda battle through the media as much as it was a military one on the ground. There were horrors on all sides. The above description is of French TV making positive publicity for the Biafran war effort, which would not have been possible for them to secure without the help of the Spiritan Missionaries on the ground, who were committed to their own parishioners in Biafra at the time. Denis Kennedy makes no secret of his allegiance. 'Twelve days later the war was over, and we were a beaten and battered nation. The Biafran army had held out magnificently for over two years, with their troops entrenched opposite the Nigerians on all fronts, and the roads and pathways mined, and tank trapped. They suffered huge casualties, but it was the lack of food and ammunition that finally caused the collapse.'[68]

....

67   Fr Denis Kennedy, C.S.Sp., *Memories of the Biafran War, July 1967-January 1970*, privately printed at Exaktaprint, Dun Laoghaire, 2018, p. 25.
68   Ibid. p. 30.

In February 1970, 27 Irish missionaries who had been expelled from Nigeria were met at Dublin Airport by large crowds, estimated in 'hundreds' and 'thousands' (depending on the newspaper), as well as by representatives of the President and Taoiseach of Ireland.

Such events take on a different complexion in hindsight and on reading 'confidential' State papers published in January 1997. These consist primarily of letters from the Irish Embassy in Lagos to the Department of Foreign Affairs in Dublin.

A 'Restricted' order applies to some documents, but those made available are often remarkably direct. For instance, in a 'Secret' letter to the then Secretary of the Department of External Affairs, Mr H.J. McCann, the Irish Ambassador to Nigeria, Mr Paul Keating, wrote in March 1970 about the returned and feted missionaries. 'We in Ireland, of course, think that the missionaries were unjustly persecuted, imprisoned and expelled under humiliating circumstances ... Nigerian public opinion and large sections of the administration of Nigerian Catholicism, and even in some cases Irish missionaries, take a different point of view. They feel that the Holy Ghost Fathers were impertinent busybodies from abroad who involved themselves in the internal affairs of Nigeria and by their propaganda and aid and comfort to the Biafrans unduly prolonged the war and caused great suffering to the Nigerian people.'

In a letter of 25th February, 1970 the ambassador criticised comments by returned Irish priests on the Nigerian leadership, particularly General Gowon, as 'fatuous emotionalism and self- advertisement', which were 'extremely unfair', as the general had been 'a moderating force'. [69]

Again, the actual historical realities are impossible to ascertain. There are so many first-hand accounts by witnesses who were on the spot, but no convincing overall narrative. We do have to take account of the

69 Patsy McGarry, commenting on documentation released into the public domain after thirty years, 'Ambassador forthright in criticism of Irish missionaries in Nigeria', *The Irish Times*, Friday, 3rd January, 1997.

cautionary tale which suggests that we were reading our own story into a quite different situation and taking over responsibilities where none were required of us. There could be a condescending patronisation, a self-appointed king-making grandiosity, which reinvents colonialism.

The last sounds on Biafran radio, it is said, were Irish rebel music.

VIII

Where to Next?

The Nightingale

The emperor of China's garden was remarkable, and it extended so far that the gardener himself did not know where it ended. In one of the trees lived a nightingale, who sang beautifully. Travellers from every country in the world came to the city, which they admired very much, but when they heard the nightingale, they all declared it to be the best of all. When the emperor heard this he exclaimed, 'What is this? I know nothing of any nightingale. Is there such a bird in my empire? And even in my garden? I have never heard of it.' He summoned all the great personages of his court but they had heard nothing of it. So he sent them off looking for the nightingale. At last they met with a poor little girl in the kitchen, who said, 'Oh, yes, I know the nightingale quite well; indeed, she can sing.' So she went into the wood where the nightingale sang, and half the court followed her. 'There she is,' said the girl, pointing to a little grey bird perched on a bough.

'Is it possible?' said the lord-in-waiting, 'a little, plain, simple thing like that.'

'Shall I sing before the emperor?' asked the nightingale, who thought he was present. 'My excellent little nightingale,' said the courtier, 'I have the great pleasure of inviting you to a court festival this evening, where you will gain imperial favour by your charming song.'

'My song sounds best in the green wood,' said the bird; but still she came willingly when she heard the emperor's wish.

The palace was elegantly decorated for the occasion. In the centre of the great hall, a golden perch had been fixed for the nightingale to sit on. The whole court was present, and the little kitchen-maid had received permission to stand by the door. All were in full dress, and every eye was turned to the little grey bird when the emperor nodded to her to begin. The nightingale sang so sweetly that the tears came into the emperor's eyes, and then rolled down his cheeks.

The nightingale's visit was most successful. She was now to remain at court, to have her own cage, with liberty to go out twice a day, and once during the night. Twelve servants were appointed to attend her on these occasions, who each held her by a silken string fastened to her leg.

One day the emperor received a large packet on which was written 'The Nightingale'. It was a work of art contained in a casket, an artificial nightingale made to look like a living one, and covered all over with diamonds, rubies and saphires. As soon as the artificial bird was wound up, it could sing like the real one, and could move its tail up and down, which sparkled with silver and gold. When it sang it was as successful as the real bird; besides, it was so much prettier to look at, for it sparkled like bracelets and breast-pins. No one noticed the real nightingale as she flew out the open window, back to her own green woods.

'What strange conduct,' said the emperor, when her flight had been discovered; and all the courtiers blamed her and said she was a very ungrateful creature. 'But we have the best bird after all,' said one, and then they would have the bird sing again, although it was the thirty-fourth time they had listened to the same piece. And after this the real nightingale was banished from the empire, and the artificial bird placed on a silk cushion close to the emperor's bed.

One evening, when the artificial bird was singing its best, and the emperor lay in bed listening to it, something inside the bird sounded 'whizz'. Then a spring cracked. 'Whir-r-r-r' went all the wheels, running round and then the music stopped. The emperor immediately sprang out of bed and called for his physician; but what could he do? Now there was great sorrow, as the bird could only be allowed to play once a year; and even that was dangerous for the works inside it. Five years passed and then a real grief came upon the land. The Chinese really were fond of their emperor, and he now lay so ill that he was not expected to live. A window stood open, and the moon shone in upon the emperor and the artificial bird. 'Music! Music!' shouted the emperor. 'You little precious golden bird, sing, pray sing! I have given you gold and costly presents; Sing! sing!' But the bird remained silent. There was no one to wind it up and it could not sing a note.

Death continued to stare at the emperor with his cold, hollow eyes, and the room was fearfully still. Suddenly there came through the open window the sound of sweet music. Outside, on the bough of a tree, sat the living nightingale. She had heard of the emperor's illness, and was therefore come to sing to him. And as she sung, the emperor fell into a sweet sleep. When he awoke, strengthened and restored, the sun shone brightly through the window; but not one of his servants had returned—they all believed he was dead; only the nightingale still sat beside him, and sang.

'You must always remain with me,' said the emperor. 'You shall sing only when it pleases you; and I will break the artificial bird into a thousand pieces.' 'No; do not do that,' replied the nightingale; 'the bird did very well as long as it could. Keep it here still. I cannot live in the palace, and build my nest; but let me come when I like. I will sit on a bough outside your window, in the evening, and sing to you; but you must promise me one thing.'

'Everything,' said the emperor, who, having dressed himself in his imperial robes, stood with the hand that held the heavy golden sword pressed to his heart.

'I only ask one thing,' she replied; 'let no one know that you have a little bird who tells you everything. It will be best to conceal it.' So saying, the nightingale flew away.

The servants now came in to look after the dead emperor; when, lo! there he stood, and, to their astonishment, said, 'Good morning.'[70]

....

70   Hans Christian Andersen, 'The Nightingale' first published by C.A. Reitzel in Copenhagen on 11th November, 1843 in the first volume of the first collection of *New Fairy Tales*.

Every society that plans to survive has to become an institution. So many religions, political parties, businesses have thrived for a few energetic years before collapsing into oblivion. Statistics supplied by sociologists (mostly in America) suggest that 75% of small businesses fail in their first five years and 50% of the remainder collapse by their 10th year. Small may be beautiful, but in the world in which we live it is not durable.

The Catholic Church (The Greek word καθολικός (*katholikos*) means 'universal') is the oldest religious institution in existence. It has over a billion members in almost every country in the world. So, the Roman Catholic Church inevitably developed an institutional aspect, over the 2,000 years of its existence. Although this time span is short when compared with the history of the universe, it is still significant in terms of our human history. It began in Jerusalem with a small nucleus of disciples who believed in the resurrection of Jesus. *The Acts of the Apostles* describes and suggests how this small group lived the Christian life as it was intended to be.

In the years between the historical life of Jesus Christ and the conversion of the Emperor Constantine, three hundred years later, the Church focused primarily on survival. Christianity spent its first three centuries as an outlawed organisation unable to possess property or make any great sociological impact. Some would see the connection between the Roman Empire and the Church as providential; others would see it as betrayal of the original message.

After the ban was lifted by the Emperor, the Church's private property grew quickly through donations from pious and wealthy people. The Lateran Palace was the first significant donation, given by Constantine himself. From the fourth century, this Palace of the Lateran on Piazza San Giovanni became the principal residence of the Popes for the next thousand years.

For nearly all of that first 1,000 years, the Catholic Church presided over the total life of Christendom and animated its laws, customs, literature, art and architecture. If you were a Christian in Europe, you belonged to the Catholic Church. Any Christianity other than the Catholic Church was a heresy, not a denomination. And this also meant that for the first thousand years of Christianity there was no 'Roman Catholicism' as we know it today, simply because our present understanding of it is coloured by its opposition to rivals who did not then exist. At that time, there was no Orthodoxy or Protestantism from which to distinguish Roman Catholicism. There was only, with a very few exceptions, the 'one, holy, Catholic and Apostolic Church' affirmed by the early creeds. This was the body of Christian believers all over the world, united by common traditions, beliefs, church structure and worship. If we had been as careful about the first of these so-called 'hall-marks' of the Church as we were about the last, we might have done more to preserve the unity which is vaunted as such an essential feature of Christianity, echoing Christ's insistent plea to the Father: 'that they may all be one. As you, Father, are in me and I am in you, may they also be in us, so that the world may believe that you have sent me.'[71]

> Institutional religion, and certainly Christianity the religion, is always a human construct. It is itself a work of human hands and manned [sic] by ordinary men and women who are no more gifted by the grace of God than the rest of us ... Christians must recognise the fact that they have regularly distorted the truth of the faith of Jesus, in various ways and to varying degrees over virtually the whole history of their religion.[72]

The idea of a 'pope' did not exist at first, although, from the beginning, there were prominent Church leaders whose authority was recognised, mostly because they were, or had known, the first disciples of Jesus. There was no unique central authority. It was not until several centuries after Christ's death that the Church began to develop into the 'Roman Catholic Church,' as we think of it today.

....

71 John 17:21.
72 James P. Mackey, *Christianity and Creation, The Essence of the Christian Faith and its Future among Religions*, A Systematic Theology, Continuum, New York & London, 2006, pp. 397.

The conversion of the Emperor Constantine in 318 CE prompted the Church to adopt a governmental structure mirroring the Roman Empire. Geographical provinces were ruled by governors ('bishops' in the imitative template adopted by the Church) based in the major city of each one. (ἐπίσκοποι *episkopoi* means 'overseer' in Greek). Bishops of such major cities as Jerusalem, Alexandria, Antioch, Rome and Constantinople emerged as preeminent. It was natural that Rome would eventually become the most important of these. Not only was it the capital of the empire, but it was the city where the apostles Peter and Paul had been martyred. Roman Catholicism in its identification of itself as 'apostolic' traces its history back to the original apostles, especially the apostle Peter, who is considered by Roman Catholics to have been the first pope. Every pope since then is regarded as Peter's spiritual successor. Pope Francis is, for instance, the 266th pope after Saint Peter.

The term Curia was used to designate the administrative apparatus of the Roman Catholic Church. It provides the central organisation for the correct functioning of the Church and the achievement of its mission. *Curia* in Medieval Latin meant court, in the sense of 'royal court' rather than 'court of law'. The Roman Curia can be loosely compared to cabinets in Western forms of governance. It comprises thirteen congregations led by a prefect, who is a cardinal.

The Vatican, where this centralised bureaucracy exists, is a relatively new establishment with a very ancient name. When King Victor Emmanuel II took back power from the Pope in 1870, and Rome became what it is today, Italy's capital city, some compensation was made to the Catholic Church for the loss of huge properties owned by the Church throughout the Middle Ages. The Lateran Treaty of 1929 brought the Vatican city-state into existence, providing some geographical base for Roman Catholic Church governance. These Lateran Agreements were incorporated into the Constitution of the Italian Republic in 1947. The treaty spoke of the Vatican as a new creation, and not as the remnant of the former Papal States which had extended throughout most of central Italy from 756 to 1870.

Vatican City was thus a compensating compromise to allow the Holy See the political benefits of territorial sovereignty. The treaty was signed by the Cardinal Secretary of State, Pietro Gasparri, on behalf of the Holy See and by Prime Minister Benito Mussolini on behalf of the Kingdom of Italy on 7th June, 1929. The golden pen used for the signing, later presented to *Il Duce,* was supplied by Pope Pius XI. And so the Vatican as we understand this term today was born less than a hundred years ago.

This Vatican City, officially *Stato della Città del Vaticano* (State of the City of the Vatican), is a landlocked sovereign city-state within the city of Rome itself. It has approximately 44 hectares [110 acres] and a population of about 800. The territory includes St Peter's Square, marked off from the territory of Italy by a simple white line. St Peter's Square itself is reached through the Via della Conciliazione which runs from the Tiber River to the basilica. This grand approach was constructed by Mussolini in something of a conciliatory gesture after the conclusion of the Lateran Treaty. The name 'Vatican' predates Christianity and is the name of the mountain (*Mons Vaticanus*) of which Vatican City forms a part. The former 'Vatican Fields' beside this mountain are where St Peter's Basilica, the Apostolic Palace, the Sistine Chapel and various museums were put, along with various other buildings.

The Church is a human organisation which travels through history as a dweller on this planet, even though those who belong to it believe that it is also a divinely appointed institution perennially guided by the Holy Spirit. This dichotomy allowed St Augustine, writing in the fourth and fifth century to identify two churches in one: the esoteric church of St John (the 'heart' of the Church), as distinct from the exoteric Church of St Peter (the 'head' of the Church). It was never the intention or the role of John to found a new Church, that was always Peter's charism, Augustine says:

> The Church knows two lives which have been laid down and commended to her by God. One is through faith, the other through vision. The apostle Peter personifies the first life, John

the second. The first has no place except on earth; it lasts only to the end of the present age and comes to an end in the next world. The second life has no end in the age to come, and its perfection is delayed until the end of the present age. ... To preserve the still and secret heart of the next life, John the Evangelist rested on Christ's breast: sublime knowledge proclaimed by John concerning the trinity and unity of the whole godhead, which in his kingdom we shall see face to face, but now, until the Lord comes, we must behold in a glass darkly. It was not only John who drank: the Lord himself has spread John's gospel throughout the world, so that according to each one's capacity all people may drink it.' [73]

Christ did not come to find a place for God in the world, but rather to show that the world has its place in God. So the Church as the Petrine Church, is a necessary though cumbersome outer shell for the Church as Spirit, or the Johannine Church, which is its inner mystical life of relationship with God. And this inner mystical relationship is continued throughout history between person and person.

From the second half of the thirteenth century to the first half of the fifteenth century, for example, when divisions and political rivalries were rife, when the Church was awash with antipopes, two great mystics, Julian of Norwich (1342 – 1416) and Catherine of Sienna (1347–1380), kept open the vital connection with the three Persons of the Trinity while the institutional Church was being torn apart.

But this double reality of the Church, the spiritual connection and the human, all-too-human carapace, makes it necessary for us to winnow the corn and jettison the chaff which every century of Christianity inevitably harvests. In the Parable of the Tares, Jesus tells us: 'Let both grow together until the harvest.'

....

73   St Augustine on St John's Gospel, Homily 124, 5,7.

Even at the most turbulent and scandalous moments in Church history there was always at least one person who kept the flame of 'right relationship' or 'orthodoxy' alive. Maximus the Confessor (born in 580; died in exile 13th August, 662) was one of the only Christians at the time who confessed true belief in who Jesus was, even when the pope of his day Honorius (625 to 638) was ready to condone the monothelite heresy.[74]

The Church as an institution is prone to every form of political intrigue and power-seeking corruption. Wherever human beings are vying with one another for control they are all subject to the dark forces which penetrate each one of us. 'The frontline between good and evil, as Alexander Solzhenitsyn suggests in his book *The Gulag Archipelago*, 'doesn't run between classes and parties but right through the human heart. It doesn't stay the same but varies over the years. You will find a bridgehead of goodness in a heart possessed by evil. And the most well-meaning heart contains an unassailable pocket of evil.'[75]

The Church as an historical structure must eventually disappear altogether. When the kingdom comes there will be no further need for earthly paraphernalia. The only thing that endures is love. Love began the Church and love is her only end. The Church's role is to deliver her children over to love and then disappear.

This also implies that the Catholic Church is not simply an organisation it is more properly described as an organism. That is: it is not simply constituted by the macrocosm of its totality, it is alive and well and fully present in each microcosm of itself, wherever 'two or three are gathered in my name.'[76] Here and now we constitute the Church. Let

----

74 Monothelitism is a teaching which began in Armenia and Syria in AD 633 and held considerable support during the seventh century AD before being officially condemned at the Third Council of Constantinople. It was really an extension of the monophysite position of earlier Christological arguments, hammered out in the seven councils previously mentioned. It wanted to believe that Jesus Christ had no human will of his own, but had only one divine will. Maximus and others held to the true doctrine, at great physical cost to himself, that Jesus Christ has two wills (human and divine) corresponding to his two natures.

75 Alexander Solzenitsyn, *The Gulag Archipelago*, Part 4, Chapter 1, 'The Ascent'.

76 Matthew 18:20.

us retrieve our birth right and take back the Church which we inherited and which we are.

To do this we have to abandon our temerity and our pleas of unworthiness. Either we do something daring and immediate or the whole edifice may collapse. No point in waiting for someone else to turn up, some great leader to emerge. We are the only ones here at the moment and so we're the ones we've been waiting for. Let's play a game of trains and imagine we're with Seamus Heaney on 'A Sofa in the Forties'.

All of us on the sofa in a line, kneeling
Behind each other, eldest down to youngest.
Elbows going like pistons, for this was a train[77]

The Great Train Robbery

The plan to intercept and rob the overnight Glasgow to London mail train in the early hours of 8th August, 1963 at Bridego Railway Bridge, Buckinghamshire, England was based on information of the amount of money it carried. The second carriage, behind the engine, known as the HVP (high-value packages) coach, carried large quantities of money and registered mail. Because of the summer bank holiday, the train was carrying more money than usual in its High Value Packages carriage – some 128 mailbags, weighing 2.5 tons, holding a total of £2,595,997 and ten shillings. The driver and his fireman were overpowered, and all the redundant carriages were uncoupled, which meant that the locomotive and the HVP carriage could be driven half a mile to the bridge where the bullion was unloaded.

Pope Francis seems to be trying to effect such an uncoupling as best he can but it is difficult. The old link and pin design which worked in the days of the Great Train Robbery have been replaced by much more effective and resistant AAR-type knuckle couplers patented in the Vatican.

....
77   Seamus Heaney, *Opened Ground*, London, Faber and Faber, 1998, p. 397.

The carriages are joined to the engine almost inflexibly. The Vatican and the Church have become identified.

A few years ago, in the course of a long railway journey, I was suddenly seized by a desire to make a tour of the little country in which I was locked up for three days, cradled in that rattle that is like the sound of pebbles rolled over and over by the waves; and I got up out of my berth. At one in the morning I went through the train in all its length. I made my way along those passages, stepping over sprawling bodies and peering into the carriages. In the dim glow cast by the night-lamps into these barren and comfortless compartments I saw a confused mass of people churned about by the swaying of the train, the whole thing looking and smelling like a barrack-room.

I sat down face-to-face with one couple. Between the man and the woman a child had hollowed himself out a place and fallen asleep. He turned in his slumber, and in the dim lamplight I saw his face. What an adorable face! This is a musician's face. This is the child Mozart. This is a life full of beautiful promise. Protected, sheltered, cultivated, what could not this child become? When by mutation a new rose is born in a garden, all the gardeners rejoice. They isolate the rose, tend it, foster it. But there is no gardener for people. This little Mozart will be shaped like the rest by the common stamping machine. This little Mozart is condemned. I went back to my sleeping car. I said to myself: Their fate causes these people no suffering. It is not an impulse to charity that has upset me like this. I am not weeping over an eternally open wound. Those who carry the wound do not feel it. It is the human race and not the individual that is wounded here, is outraged here. I do not believe in pity. What torments me tonight is the gardener's point of view. What torments me is not this poverty to which after all one can accustom oneself as easily as to sloth. What torments me is not the humps nor the hollows nor the ugliness. It is the sight, a little bit in all these people, of Mozart murdered. Only the Spirit, if it breathe upon the clay, can create persons.[78]

....
78   Antoine de Saint-Exupery, *Wind, Sand and Stars,* Chapter 10 – Conclusion.

Three carriages from the engine

How do we here in Ireland, in this twenty-first century, get nearer to our God? That is the only really important question. Answering it requires that we take a realistic and objective appraisal of our present situation, putting everything, even our most sacred and cherished beliefs, under the microscope, and preparing ourselves to take nothing whatsoever seriously except the love of God. At the moment, in our Church, we are at three removes from our goal. The Irish Roman Catholic Church is three carriages away from the engine. How do we uncouple ourselves from the two carriages which are getting in the way: the Roman and the Irish.

Christy Hannity

The first carriage, or rather the last, is a specifically Irish version of Christianity. Much of the social pathology which contaminated Ireland in the twentieth century sprang from a spiritual and moral paradigm forced upon us as an island of 'Saints and Scholars'. Some of us may have been saints or scholars or both, and more credit to them; but the majority were not; and these were damaged by the attempt to force them into this mould. The ideals on which we based the conduct of our lives may have been very noble but they did not represent us as we are. Unless such sociology acknowledges and integrates our full humanity, we become dislocated, schizoid, two-timers.

What became known in France, for instance, as *Le Catholicisme du Type Irlandais* was largely a product of imported nineteenth century spiritualties, emphasising personal holiness and condemning our evil human nature and untrustworthy instincts. It has been described as Irish Jansenism and it presented a grim theology, rigid, authoritarian and moralistic. It was certainly responsible for much fear, guilt and pessimism. According to World Health Organisation Statistic Reports[79] between 1961 and 1968 the Republic of Ireland had the highest hospitalisation treatment rate for mental illness in the world.

---

79   For 1961: 221-245; and 1968: 529-551.

When Nancy Scheper-Hughes's stayed for over a year in the village of An Clochán on the Dingle peninsula in 1974, she never told the villagers that she was a professor of anthropology at the University of California at Berkeley, and that they were the subjects of her study of 'pathogenic stresses that surround the coming of age in rural Ireland'. When all her conversations with people of the village during that year together were distilled and published in a book called *Saints, Scholars and Schizophrenics: Mental Illness in Rural Ireland* three years later in 1977, it caused a sensation. Cloaking the true name of the village under the moniker 'Ballybran,' and referring to the villagers, or 'parishioners', with pseudonyms, Scheper-Hughes attempted to afford them a modicum of privacy while describing their intimate relations with each other in great detail. But 'we're not all fools in this part of the country'. The strategy failed completely – not only were the villagers able to identify each other instantly upon reading the book, but the identity of the village itself was uncovered by persistent researchers and investigative journalists. Reactions ranged from 'She should be shot' to 'bad 'cess to anyone who throws good Irish pounds after a copy of that Yankee rubbish'.

Despite being widely celebrated in North American anthropological circles, the book shocked and outraged many of those who were its subjects: the people of An Clochán took offense at what they perceived to be a breach of trust, an illicit airing of secrets about their sexuality, mental and emotional health, and family life which they had confided to Sheper-Hughes in private conversations. 'There is a difference,' the author was told, 'between whispering something beside a fire or across a counter and seeing it printed for the world to see. It becomes a public shame.'

Twenty-five years later, with the publication of the 20th anniversary edition of the book, Sheper-Hughes returned to a hostile reception in the village. She was still trying to resolve the conflict between her professional duties as a psychological anthropologist and her personal responsibility towards the people of An Clochán. The intimacy of the study was necessitated by Scheper-Hughes's concentration on family relations, which she sees as profoundly implicated in the emergence of schizophrenia among the community's most vulnerable members.

The subject of her book alone would have been enough to raise eyebrows in many circles in Ireland. Basically she suggests that the World Health Organisation statistics reporting Ireland to have the highest proportion of hospital treatment for mental illness in the world during the 1960s were connected to family relationships and religious scruples. Sheper-Hughes makes no bones about it: two categories of siblings are especially prone: the son singled out for the vocation to the priesthood with all the challenges and difficulties that such a pathway entailed, but worse off was the son on whom the burden of succession fell. The tendency towards schizophrenia is especially pronounced among the young and middle-aged 'bachelor farmers,' who had been coerced by their families into remaining in the village of their birth and taking over their fathers' farms in an age where farming had lost its once high status as a profession and had become economically unprofitable in all but a few cases.

The study identified the breakdown of the traditional extended family structure, along with the emigration of many of the eligible young women from rural Irish villages, as the reasons why these men were living in social isolation, loneliness and mostly unwanted celibacy. The cause of this unfulfilling lifestyle was the brutal socialisation process, in which the perceived 'runt' of a family is demoralised, scapegoated, and made to feel overwhelmingly guilty if he refuses to remain at home to tend to his aging parents and inherit the family farm.

The possibility of course is that if Nancy Sheper-Hughes had carried out her research in any part of rural Ireland at the time, she might have found similar patterns and come to the same conclusions. Many might have been similarly outraged by her importunacy and brazenness, but some might have recognised the truth of her findings as did one of the escapees from Ballybran. He wrote back to his distraught mother saying: 'and you can tell Da that '*that* book' is the first one to speak the truth about this secret Ireland of ours.' At least one other person recorded that reading this book changed her mindset completely. Until then she herself (and the parish at large) viewed her decision to give up a disapproved 'love match' in order to stay at home and care for her widowed father and unmarried brothers as the good, moral, 'Christian' thing to do. As was said in the village: 'her father and brothers "had a right to claim her".' She was happy and relieved to hear an alternative view of her situation.

Brendan Kennelly in his 1991 *The Book of Judas*[80] refers to our Irish version of Christianity as Christy Hannity ('an epileptic fish-and-chip shitkicker from Tralee') whose motto is: 'Pretend to be what they believe you are/ You are what they believe they think' [333].

> I have this vision of the world as a man
> With mean eyes and a hideous jollity in his voice
> I smell his heart, his guts, I absorb his rot.
>
> In spite of that, on certain days I see
> This odious contraption is preferable to me.

Perhaps it is evidence of both the strength and the weakness of 'Irish Catholicism' John Jordan suggests, 'that it may evoke a gamut of responses ranging from savage indignation through resigned embarrassment to ecstatic reverence.'[81] Even if we descend to 'the dark night of the hole' we know that even the dark or darkness is not the answer because, in reality, we discover it to be 'The Green Dark,' a self-indulgently Irish form of darkness [225].

'There is something in Irish life which demands that you over-simplify practically everything. This is another way of saying that everybody must be labelled, made readily accessible, explainable' [9]. Christianity in Ireland had developed into such a simplified version of the original

---

80 Brendan Kennelly, *The Book of Judas*, Newcastle upon Tyne, Bloodaxe, 1991. For the remainder of this section numbers in square brackets refer to this edition.

81 John Jordan, 'Irish Catholicism,' *The Crane Bag*, Volume 7, No. 2 The Forum Issue, p. 108.

that 'this culture is now in an advanced state of self-parody. Or, if you wish, in an advanced state of self-betrayal, playing Judas to itself'. The oversimplification is partly the refusal to admit the necessity of exploring our underground sewer.

> Got a job in the sewers. With
> Helmet gloves rubber clothes flashlamp
> I went down below Dublin
>
> From Kingsbridge into O'Connell Street,
> Flashin' me lamp in the eyes o' rats
> Diabolical as tomcats. Rats don't like light
> in their eyes.

Christian hypocrisy in this regard is a betrayal of essential humanity. Are we not, as Judas possibly was, 'a shrewd refuser of what might have made him loveable and vulnerable?' [11]. The fearful obstruction of an essential part of our make-up, caused by an oversimplified and sterilised version of ourselves, and the banishment of what is rejected to the hidden gloom of maligned and repudiated shadows, inevitably creates a lawless untrammelled world where parts of us live on in dangerously schizoid isolation. Kennelly sets himself the task of giving voice to this judasphere. He follows the 'Judasvoice as it appeared in words before his eyes'. He found it 'odd and ordinary, freakish and free, severed and pertinent' [10]. 'To what extent, Kennelly wonders in an interview,[82] 'have we elected Judas to be our real redeemer from the consequences of what we have ourselves created but like to blame somebody else for, when things go wrong?'

The trouble is that 'Judas is the shrewdest whore/ That ever stacked a man with a galloping disease' [19].

....

82   Interview with Ksatie Donovan, *The Irish Times*, 19th December, 1991.

Let my story feed the children
Who need a monster to hate and fear [47].

The Book of Judas 'seemed to write itself' [60] says Kennelly, about a world of adulterers, childmolesters, informers, pimps, racists, spies and terrorists. And maybe 'no image fits' [53]. What the poet is creating is 'a heady odyssey in non-existence'. The truth may be that the search for a Judasvoice is a false trail because 'you have no voice I recognise as yours/ Unless it be this laneway packed with shadows, hungers'.

Poetry is a way of truth which involves the dedicated surrender of the poet, who filters through his or her person the comprehensive uncensored variety of experience 'to achieve definition, to be purified by the poem'.

In the Preface to his *Selected Poems*[83] of 1969 Kennelly described some of his work as 'an attempt to express some kind of personal philosophy,' to 'try to define the nature of personal vision'. Twenty years later in his 1990 collection of selected poems, he says that the poet, as visionary, is 'riddled with different voices, many of them in vicious conflict'. The aim of the debate is to achieve a 'vision' which is no less than 'an attempt to make sense out of the world'.[84]

Ottavio Paz, the Mexican writer, who won the Nobel Prize for literature in 1990, wrote a series of 'Essays on Modern Poetry' called *The Other Voice*:

> That voice was not heeded by the revolutionary ideologues of our century, and this explains, in part at least, the cataclysmic failure of their plans. It would be disastrous if the new political philosophy were to ignore those realities that have been hidden and buried by the men and women of the Modern Age. The function of poetry for the last two hundred years has been to remind us of their existence; the poetry of tomorrow cannot do otherwise. Its mission will not be to provide new ideas but to announce what has

83   Brendan Kennelly, *Selected Poems*, Dublin, 1969, p. xii.
84   Brendan Kennelly, *A Time for Voices, Selected Poems 1960-1990*, Bloodaxe Books, 1990, p. 13.

been obstinately forgotten for centuries. Poetry is memory become image, and image become voice.[85]

What are all these explosive, antagonistic and negative reactions for the most part? They come from a fearful protective mechanism which hides the ambiguity, the treachery, the 'evil' inside ourselves. This internal mechanism works by constructing a corresponding hate object outside ourselves on which we can exorcise our panic and insecurity. We have an idealised version of ourselves and anything other than this is repressed. However, it continues to prowl the depths. Projection is the term used for throwing all the contents of that shadow onto someone else. We see and condemn in the monster outside all those weaknesses and tendencies which we fail to acknowledge or accept inside ourselves.

In the Irish Catholic psyche such hate objects or scape-goats, upon which it was acceptable, even encouraged, to expend any amount of hatred were, for instance, Satan, Judas and Oliver Cromwell. These became enlarged caricatures, the projected parasites, of the repressed aspect of ourselves, what Brian Friel called *The Enemy Within* in his play about St Columba, the archetypal paragon of Irish virtue. We have an idealised version of ourselves as we should be, and Columba is one of the role models for such perfection. The rest is repressed. Such repression is more than suppression. It is more than denying or controlling urges or impulses which we actually feel in ourselves. Repression is refusing even to acknowledge the existence of such realities. The mere entertainment of them would be too shameful to tolerate with self-respect.

Repression pushes even the memory of such thoughts and feelings into oblivion. An unmarried person, for instance, who believes that any thought of sexual intercourse outside of marriage is immoral may repress these sexual urges consciously until they are seemingly obliterated. However, at the unconscious level they continue to live a life of their own, which may manifest itself in

85   Ottavio Paz, *The Other Voice, Essays on Modern Poetry*, Translated by Helen Lane, Harcourt, Brace, Jovanovich, 1991, pp. 150-155.

hysterical condemnation of sexual indulgence in others. This sanitizing process, whereby everything that is deemed unworthy of a human being is wiped out, leads to condemnation of others who fail to achieve this profile.

For Catholic-Gaelic Ireland the most obvious hate-figures are Oliver Cromwell and Judas Iscariot. They are embedded in every Irish psyche as the ultimate oppressor, defector and traitor. Each one received the full extent of Brendan Kennelly's scrutiny in 1983 and 1991 respectively. His obsession with otherness, with introducing himself and ourselves to the 'enemy' we are meant to learn how to love, finds its most demanding and appropriate protagonists in the archetypal enemy and the icon of apostasy in the Roman Catholic Irish psyche:

> I don't think any Irishman is complete as an Irishman until he becomes an Englishman, imaginatively speaking. I was reared to hate and fear Cromwell, the legends, the folklore of my own parish, the unquestioning hatred of him, which was then transferred to England. That appalled me when I began to try to think ... Cromwell is an ordinary experiment in my own psyche: that I am giving voice to a man who made trees wither. The worst thing you can say in the part of the country I grew up in is 'the curse of Cromwell on you' and I wanted to turn that curse into a blessing.[86]

As always, Brendan Kennelly describes the success of his venture in a story:

> I got a punch in the jaw one night crossing O'Connell Bridge from a man who said 'Aren't you the bastard that had a good word for him! Aren't you the fellow that's making a hero out of him?' ... And I said, 'No, he's a man, you're a man, I'm a man'. And he said: 'Drogheda!' He had all the clichés ... All of us are victims of clichés we don't even begin to suspect.

---

86   Interview of Brendan Kennelly by Richard Pine, *Irish Literary Supplement*, Spring 1990, p. 22.

With Cromwell behind him and after eight years of 'clearing a space' within himself, he lets us hear the voice of Judas. This sounds forth in a 378 page epic. We have to marvel at the almost unlimited capacity of this poet to act as ventriloquist, using the word in its original Latin sense of 'speaking from the belly', to evacuate:

> And clear a space for himself
> Like Dublin city on a Sunday morning
> About six o'clock
> Dublin and myself are rid of our traffic then
> And I am walking. [87]

This further task of unearthing the aboriginal traitor was evisceration for the poet as he tried to haul both these monsters from the depths.

In 2009, Susan Gubar wrote what she calls a 'first' biography of Judas Iscariot from youth to old age, throughout 'the extensive span of his multimedia existence'. It is a cultural biography of one of the most famous hate objects in History: the man who betrayed Jesus Christ. She explores the work of historians, artists, novelists and scholars to give an overview of how Judas has been portrayed over the centuries by different people in various cultures. The portrait is not drawn by delineating the figure or the face of her subject but by shading in the surrounding canvas until a figure emerges. However, the strange and disturbing face that appears is not Judas Iscariot's but yours and mine.

The biography is ours as much as his, from the first century to the twenty-first. She puts on display the various representations, visual, literary, theatrical, cinematic, even musical, of Judas Iscariot and comments incisively on each.

The book is not so much a biography as a litany of the worst we think about ourselves, and which we then gather up like spitting mambas and

87   Brendan Kennelly, *A Time For Voices: Selected Poems 1960-1990*, Bloodaxe, 1990, p. 124.

hurl at the hate object we have placed in the stocks of our collective imaginations. Projection is a most profound and subtle psychological process which colors much of what we do and say. It is difficult to detect because of its hidden nature. It is, we are told, the fundamental mechanism by which we keep ourselves misinformed about ourselves. These hidden instinctual defence-mechanisms are rotating catapults, aimed and loaded, which we use to batter to death our own worst fears about ourselves. Whatever we find threatening or unacceptable about our deepest feelings we repress and then attribute to someone else. Most of us have our own personal Aunt Sally whom we pillory for all we are worth and blame for our shortcomings and misfortunes. Here we are presented with a universally approved object of our wrath, and we can watch in detail the catalogue of missiles we have hurled at him over the centuries. The litany provides an image of how ghastly we ourselves are, and how devastating are our catapulting mechanisms of insult and injury, our destructive psychological reflexes. Susan Gubar has amassed a huge, brutish, repulsive catalogue of how Christian imagination has vented its spleen on the disciple who betrayed Jesus. Even more disturbingly she demonstrates how Judas became identified with 'Jewry' which then took on the torture inflicted on a people accused of being God-betrayers and God-killers.

His name in Hebrew, Yehuda, is what the Israelite kingdom is also called, from which the very word 'Judaism' derives. The ugly face of anti-Semitism appears in most depictions of Judas Iscariot throughout history. He has become the scapegoat for our deepest most atavistic and racist tendencies. If Judas never existed, our psyches would have had to invent him to carry the burden of our self-hatred. Gubar shows how slender the evidence is and how tiny the basis for such a mountain of prejudice. New Testament accounts, although minimal in themselves, were sufficient to give *carte blanche* to succeeding ages to vent their bile. Reading what Martin Luther and even Karl Barth wrote about Judas is stomach-churning stuff.

Gubar reads Kennelly as a prophetic voice describing Christy Hannity as it emerged in Ireland during the twentieth century. Christy became an institutionalised embodiment of the spirit of Judas rather than the spirit of Jesus. Everywhere in our churches, our schools, our banks, our politics, our legal, family, trade-union, communications and cultural systems, the Judas-effect of greed, avarice and betrayal are more in evidence, as recognisable hall-marks, than are the ethos of the Sermon on the Mount.

We need a relationship with God and an understanding of Christianity which would correspond to and connect with the reality of who we are. Artists have always claimed to be in touch with the people, their art found its source in this reality, which was often the reason why it was condemned in the past. The dialogue between who we are and who Christ is should lead us to a fuller and more comprehensive way of being.

The Last Italian Carriage

The 'Roman' part of that Irish Roman Catholic trio of carriages is more difficult to disengage. The year 1850 saw two events that occasioned the centralisation and Romanisation of the Irish Catholic church. The first was the appointment of Paul Cullen to the vacant primatial see of Armagh; the second was the National Synod of Thurles – the first of its kind in Ireland since the twelfth century.[88] Cullen had lived and worked in Rome for thirty years and was determined to make the Catholic church in Ireland in the image and likeness of the church in Rome, thus making him responsible for what has been called our 'Cullenisation'.

> Was it for this the wild geese spread
> The grey wing upon every tide;
> For this that all that blood was shed,
> For this Edward Fitzgerald died,
> And Robert Emmet and Wolfe Tone,

---

88   John J. Ó Riordáin, C.SS.R. *Irish Catholics, Tradition and Transition*, Dublin, Veritas, 1980, pp. 70.

All that delirium of the brave?
Romantic Ireland's dead and gone,
It's with O'Leary in the grave.

— W.B. Yeats, 'September 1913'

The Fenian revolutionary so admired by Yeats, John O'Leary, described Cullen as 'one of the most dogmatic, domineering, and self-willed of men, with much of what he took to be, and what in a sense was, religion, but with apparently no feeling for his country other than that it was a good Catholic machine, fashioned mainly to spread the faith over the world.' When the Archbishop of Toronto in 1864 sent a circular to the Irish hierarchy revealing the real state and condition of Irish Catholic emigrants in his diocese, revelations of wretched poverty, criminality and abandonment of faith, O'Leary wrote that it was 'a strong commentary upon a supposed saying of Archbishop Cullen's, that the famine of '45 was a dispensation of Providence, to drive the Irish abroad to spread the Catholic faith'.[89]

The *Irish Ecclesiastical Record,* a monthly journal founded by Cullen in 1864, promoted his ultramontane views.[90] The journal's motto was supposedly taken from 'the sayings of St Patrick' as recorded in The Book of Armagh: *Ut Christiani ita et Romani sitis* (as you are children of Christ, so be you children of Rome).

The Synod of Thurles would, in the words of Cullen who was present there in his dual capacity as leader of the Irish hierarchy and apostolic delegate of Pope Pius IX, 'lay the foundation of a good and general system of Canon Law for the Irish Church'. We have to remember also the wider climate of the nineteenth century in Europe which was a time of centralisation, standardisation and vigorous administration. The states

89   John O'Leary, *Recollections of Fenians and Fenianism* (2 vols., London, 1896), ii, 31.
90   When a non-Italian was elected to the papacy, he was said to be *papa ultramontano,* that is, a pope from beyond the mountains, namely the Alps. The term came to imply a clerical political tendency within the Catholic Church that places strong emphasis on the prerogatives and powers of the Pope.

of Germany were fused into the new German Empire and the states of Italy came together to form one kingdom. The Church of Rome followed suit: there was increased centralisation around the infallible pope and increased standardisation in liturgical practice and canon law. Eskimos, Congolese, Bengalis and Samoans were baptised using Latin formulae, and Mass was said in Latin using the rite which was identical in every parish of the Roman Catholic world.

Ireland has often had fraught relationships with Rome, from the time Pope Celestine sent Patrick in the fifth century to convert the barbarian Irish. There are, of course, as many views of St Patrick as there are Irish people who chain him to their cause. Some theologians see him as the one who converted the Irish to Holy Roman Christianity, others portray him as a failed proselytiser, one who came to conquer but succumbed to the subtle charm of the Celts.

James Mackey is one such iconoclast. He points out that Patrick makes it quite clear in the only writings of his available to us that the Irish he came to evangelise were '*barbaras itaque gentes*, a barbarian people that worshipped *idola et immunda*, idols and unclean things'. In other words, he saw the Irish as ignorant unworthies and their religion as insufferable paganism. His task was to expunge and replace. 'In his own mind, he set about supplanting their satanic myths and cults with the one, true religion.'[91]

However, as Mackey further suggests, historical circumstance thwarted his colonial idealism. The Irish certainly did take to the religion he was promoting but not in the way he was hoping. Patrick's 'Christianity' was a tainted product. It had already been steeped in centuries of Greek thought and Roman culture to be almost indistinguishable from these trappings. Ireland had never been conquered by Rome, had never been part of the Roman Empire. Truth be told, the Romans hardly deemed it worth the effort.

The constantly overheard cliché about 'seven hundred years of persecution' for Irish Catholics needs to be seriously diluted. Irish

91   James P. Mackey, *Christianity and Creation, The Essence of the Christian Faith and its Future among Religions*, A Systematic Theology, Continuum, New York & London, 2006, pp. 397.

Catholicism as we know it today, dates from the sixteenth or seventeenth century. The Reformation, especially in its English incarnation, produced in Ireland the paranoid, insular, nationalistic version of Catholicism which came to fruition in the twentieth century. Before this, everyone involved in persecuting us, with a few notable exceptions, were also Catholics.

The Anglo-Saxon conquest of Britain in the sixth century and the Frankish conquest of Gaul, meant that the Irish church was cut off from Rome for at least a hundred years and left to its own development and devices. This allowed it to express itself distinctively in the great monastic foundations which gave it a unique cultural identity in the sixth and seventh centuries. The flourishing of Clonard, Clonfert, Derry, Kildare and Lismore, among others, allowed native rules to be drawn up for all such monastic foundations. Not a single continental religious order was established in Ireland for the first five centuries of Christianity. Ireland developed its own particular brand. The outstanding figure of this native variety was Columba of Iona, from whose influence the Celtic version of Christianity spread further afield.

It was only after Columba's death in 597 that a Benedictine monk, Augustine, who was prior of a monastery in Rome, was sent to England by Pope Gregory the Great to 'convert' the English. He is regarded as the founder of the English church. Without him and another English Abbot of Ripon, Wilfred, the influence of Columba might have spread throughout England. This was the first of many attempts by Rome 'to check deviationist tendencies in the Irish Church'.[92] At the Synod of Whitby in 664, the Irish monks were accused by Wilfred of preferring the authority of Columba to that of the See of Peter. By the year 800 the Irish had been brought to heel. This meant that the Church in Ireland, with the See of Armagh recognised as the supreme ecclesiastical authority, had conformed to all the practices of the Universal Church guided by Rome. Even commentators sympathetic to Irish idiosyncrasy regarded all this as

92   John Jordan, 'Irish Catholicism,' *The Crane Bag*, Vol. 7, no. 2, 1983, p. 106.

necessary and appropriate on account of 'the tenacious particularism' of Irish communities and 'the almost incredible confidence they reposed in the absolute validity of some of their own insular traditions'.

By the twelfth century the Irish church was again in trouble with Rome. The battle was about Roman imposition of the Rule of St Benedict over the local preference for the Rule of Columba or some other native monastic legislator. The reform which again brought the Irish church in line was instigated by St Malachy, born in Armagh in 1095. He, more than anyone, was responsible for integrating the Irish church into the norms of the universal Roman church. In 1139 he travelled to Rome to secure official confirmation for the dioceses of Armagh and Cashel. The church in Ireland had been in existence for over six hundred years before Rome appointed an official legate to the country in the person of Gillebert of Limerick. On his way to Rome, Malachy visited Bernard of Clairvaux who sent back to Ireland with him a number of Cistercian monks to found the abbey of Mellifont. Bernard wrote a life of Malachy wherein he describes the Irish he was trying to rule: 'he had been appointed not to human beings but to wild beasts.'

Hooked on hierarchy

What we need is 'a paradigm shift to something more closely resembling the church of the first millennium, an "inverted pyramid" in which the People of God are primary and priests, religious, bishops, popes have to exercise their leadership roles in service and together with others.'[93]

Hierarchy is a paradigm which remains endemic to anything Roman, and it will require much resilience and ingenuity to remove it as a brand mark from those who follow Jesus Christ in the Catholic Church.

Where does it spring from? One of the more influential books in the formation of our Western mindsets is *The Celestial and Ecclesiastical Hierarchies* written by someone quite recently entitled Pseudo-Dionysius

93 Gerry O'Hanlon, 'Church and State in a Changing Environment,' *The Furrow*, September, 2019, p. 505.

the Areopagite. His writings had the status of apostolic authority until the nineteenth century, and are still regarded as ranking among the classics of western spirituality. Some of this reputation stems from the intrinsic value of the texts he wrote, and the philosophical and theological genius of their author, but it has to be said that most of it is the result of blatant chicanery resulting in a fifteen hundred years of deception and fraud. Presenting himself as Dionysius the Areopagite, a disciple of St Paul mentioned in Acts 17:34, the author of these works lived at some point in the sixth century and belonged to a neo-platonic tradition which sought to have authoritative influence on Christianity. Such pseudonymous piracy was nothing unusual at the time. If I wrote a thriller I signed it Frederick Forsythe or with a whodunit I would pass it off as Agatha Christie and nobody bothered to check the credentials. These sixth century writings were published as the work of an early disciple of St Paul and therefore attained a status of apostolic authority. Later writers, such as Thomas Aquinas, dared not question the teachings of so eminent a predecessor. It was also a sure-fire marketing ploy. Any book by so reliable a personage was guaranteed best-seller status in the foreseeable future.

It was only in the nineteenth century that scientific and pedantic historical scholarship called the Areopagite's bluff. But he already had fourteen centuries of celebrity to his name and had made his mark on Medieval mindsets. Being stamped as a 'pseud' two hundred years ago was small change for this remarkably successful thirteen hundred year hoax. And, like many a fake in the world of literature he became far more famous than the person he was pretending to be.

The Pseudo-Denis or Dionysius does have many very pertinent and wonderful insights, but his essentially Neoplatonic world-view rests upon the following shape-shifting principle: that the ultimate source of all reality is 'the One', an utterly simple, ineffable, unknowable subsistence which is both the creative source and the teleological end of all existing things.

From this inexpressible 'one' the rest of the universe issues as a sequence of ever-diminishing lesser beings, each one following and remaining less important, and therefore established as a distinctive notch under the one before it. He had the distinction of listing and describing all those ever-diminishing notches both in heaven and on earth from the top of the pyramid to the lowliest base. Such an archetype and structure had a lasting effect on our psyches and provided a determining model for all classification of reality. It has since dominated Roman systematisation to the point of almost becoming its signature. Church authorities in Rome have remained inordinately obsessed by hierarchical structure, while the rest of the world has moved on towards more egalitarian horizons.

Whatever is proposed to central government in Rome, in terms of improvement or modification, must translate into such preconceived paradigms, must become three-layered, cordoned off, sub-divided. This 'traditional shape' and recognisable protocol must be adapted to your scheme otherwise it won't fit. Much time is spent working out who precedes whom in processional etiquette. But, essentially this means imposing structures which Rome regards as obvious and necessary, but which, to a contemporary sensibility, appear obsolete and irrelevant. Such categories dictate essential divisions between men and women, clerics and lay people. They also involve an almost fetishist categorisation into three descending orders.

Cardinals come in packets of three: Cardinal Protector, Cardinal Vicar or Crown Cardinal. Bishops too can be Titular, Coadjutor or Auxiliary. The lowest possible form of entitlement in this hierarchical sacerdotal scale is Monsignor - a customary or honorary title belonging to a prelate, or granted to individuals who have rendered valuable service to the Church, or who provide some special function in Church governance. Pope Francis, in a despairing attempt to declutter, suspended the title of Monsignor except to members of the Holy See's diplomatic service.

Even in heaven you have, according to the celestial hierarchies, three kinds of angel: the Cherubim, the Seraphim and the Thrones; and if you plan to be a saint you accede to this preeminent state by travelling through three orders of righteousness: the venerable, those who are on the way; the beatified who are almost there, and the canonised, who have finally and definitively made it into the premier league.

Under the leadership of ultramontanist Cardinal Cullen from 1852 until 1878, the Irish Catholic Church assumed a form that it maintained for over a century. Characterised by strong allegiance to Rome its vast institutional presence took control of Catholic education, health and welfare homes. The exceptional popular piety of twentieth-century Ireland sprang from Cullen's success in standardising Irish devotional and liturgical life along Roman lines.

Back to our train journey: between the Irish carriage modelled on Columba and his ascetic profile, and the Roman carriage interiorly decorated by Cardinal Cullen we need to do some spring cleaning. Uncoupling the unnecessary could allow for retrieval of the essential.

IX

Makeover Melchisedech

The Roman Catholic Church has a heap of decluttering to do before it can even begin to emulate the basic message of its founder. Let us begin with the wardrobe. Traditional clerical dress is derived from clothes worn by fashionable personages in ancient Rome. As fashions changed the tendency towards conservatism caused the Church to retain the original selection. Symbolic meanings have been applied which fail to justify the more practical decision to use such clothing in the first place.

An example is the 'cassock' which became the 'ordinary' dress of priests. It derived from a warm, long-armed garment worn by pre-Christian Celts known as a *Caracalla*. Fashionable Romans despised such vulgar barbarian dress until the Emperor Marcus Aurelius Antonius (121-180) decided to wear one to make himself more popular with his troops. Overnight it became high fashion. *Caracalla* became 'cassock' in English and it should 'ideally', when closed at the front, have thirty-three buttons for Roman Catholic clergy, symbolising each of the thirty-three years of Jesus' human life on earth, or thirty-nine buttons for Anglican clergy, symbolising the thirty-nine Articles of Religion.[94]

There are certain items of clothing which everyone knows should go, despite the reluctance of antiquarians and hoarders to say goodbye. Some irrelevant fripperies are harmless enough, others represent the contrary opposite to everything Christianity was constituted to proclaim. Ruthlessness is the only response. We gotta get rid of the crazy makers. I give only one example.

....

94   Richard Taylor, *How to Read a Church*, Random House, London, 2003, p. 228.

The Cappa Magna

The *cappa magna* (literally, 'great cape') is a 20-yard long ecclesiastical garment with a long train which can only be worn by cardinals, bishops and certain other honorary prelates. Its colour for cardinals is red and for bishops violet. Cardinals and Papal Nuncios are entitled to wear a *cappa magna* of watered silk. Not, strictly speaking, a liturgical vestment but rather a travelling overcoat, it is what these dignitaries might wear while entering a church or cathedral. If they are attending rather than celebrating, they may continue to wear it 'in choir' where there may be enough room for its seven-metre long silken train with accompanying hood lined with ermine in winter and silk in summer. Originally designed to cover the back and hindquarters of a horse, its purpose was to prevent passers-by from witnessing the droppings which might emerge from the cardinal's steed if the latter at any moment along the way were to relieve itself suddenly. The customary steaming globules associated with equine defecation would take from the required dignity of a cardinal and might even cause unseemly titters from unruly peasants unaccustomed to such effortless profusion.

Altar servers hold up the train which often can stretch to the width of the sanctuary while the wearer reverences the altar to makes his way to wherever seating arrangements have been indicated. If the prelate is to feature as celebrant he makes an about turn and heads for the sacristy, where the voluminous cape is removed and stored while appropriate liturgical attire for celebrating sacramentally is put on: the dalmatic of charity, the stole of pardon and the chasuble of mercy, each symbolising his role as high priest *in persona Christi*.

Aficionados will insist that this para-liturgical ceremonial provides powerful symbolic testimony to the fact that the world's prestige should have no place at the altar.

Bearers of the *Cappa Magna* are entitled to wear on their heads a *galero* (plural: *galeri*) which is a broad-brimmed hat with tessellated strings at either side. Few have the courage these days to sport such headgear, which makes them look like a cross between the Mask of Zorro and an advertisement for sherry, but the *galero* continues its appearance as part of ecclesiastical heraldry. This softer ecclesiastical headgear replaces the helmet or crest considered too aggressive and belligerent for men of the cloth. The colour of the *galero* and the number of tassels involved indicate the place of the wearer on the hierarchical ladder. Bishops generally use a green *galero* with six green tassels on each side; archbishops sport ten green tassels on each side; while cardinals have fifteen red tassels on each side of a red hat. Chinese bishops avoid the green *galero* in their coat of arms, this colour suggesting in that country that the bearer is a cuckold.

The boy stood on the burning deck

In October 2008, I was elected fifth abbot of Glenstal Abbey in County Limerick. It was a shock to me but, I think, more of a shock to the community who elected me. Monasteries don't have election campaigns so you never really know who is likely to be a candidate until the thirty or so members assemble in a room and the first straw vote is taken. The person elected has to receive two thirds of the votes cast before he can be elected abbot.

Since I had done nothing to make this happen and the result was so unwarranted and unlikely, I had to presume it was the work of the Holy Spirit and so I accepted. However, I soon discovered that this vote of our community could not be ratified by 'the authorities' in Rome, unless I, who had been a brother monk for almost fifty years, was prepared to be ordained to the priesthood.

The President of our Congregation, Ansgar Schmidt, who had come from Germany to supervise the election, had been in the same situation himself. He had been elected abbot of his community and had to be ordained to take up this position. He told me not to bother trying to change the rules. He had tried every possible loophole to avoid ordination, but in the end realised that it was pointless. I was sixty-four, the oldest abbot ever elected by the Glenstal community and most of my reasons for not wanting to be ordained in the first place had either faded or diminished. I never wanted to be either a priest or a member of the establishment of the Roman Catholic Church. My search for God, which has been lifelong and obsessional, was allowed the untrammelled freedom it required by taking the three Benedictine vows of Obedience, Stability, and *Conversatio Morum* in 1964.

One month later I was ordained a priest by the Archbishop of Cashel and Emly, Dermot Clifford, on the feast of the Immaculate Conception, 8th December, 2008. That day the great Turkish oak outside Ballyneale House, which was almost as wide as it was tall, was blown down in a storm. The slip from this tree, which my father had planted here at Glenstal Abbey on the day of my profession, was by now a well-established Turkish Oak in its own right beside the chapel lake. The farm manager at Ballyneale, Tom Fennessy, turned a wooden bowl from the fallen tree which he gave me as an ordination present. I keep it in my bedroom. I wasn't quite sure whether the storm-felled tree was approval or reproach, but I knew that the event had been registered at Knockfierna.

Examining the reasons for my ordination in order to become abbot of a small monastery in County Limerick, I was frankly stunned by the results of a very cursory preliminary investigation. I had noticed, of course, that the two abbesses elected in Benedictine houses not far from our own, were not required to receive ordination before taking up office.

As far as I could ascertain, since the year 1983, which was only thirty years before this date, a canon has been added to the Revised Code of Canon Law, the code which regulates our lives as members of the Roman Catholic Church, which stipulates that 'power' in the Church can be exercised only by those who are ordained priests. This also means, of course, that men, as only men can be ordained priests, alone have real power in the Church.

As there were no impediments to my receiving the required sacrament, I agreed to be fast-tracked to ordination. Such an anecdote in my own life raises serious problems for the Roman Catholic Church in general. I was determined to come back to this problem and examine it in greater depth once my mandate of eight years as abbot was over.

According to Ladislas Orsy, an expert in Canon Law who attended Vatican Council II as an adviser, a theological opinion about 'sacred power,' not sufficiently debated by theologians, has been incorporated into the Revised Code of Canon Law (1983), in particular in Canon 129. This canon specifies that only those who have received sacred orders are qualified for the power of governance, also called the power of jurisdiction. The canon further stipulates that although lay members of the Christian faithful can cooperate in the exercise of this same power, they cannot wield it in any significant way because, legally speaking, 'cooperate' does not mean 'participate'.[95]

This is a matter separate and different from the question of women's ordination.[96] What we are talking about here is the complete 'clericalisation' of the Church. Whether priests are men or women, or both, we cannot have a situation where only priests can exercise power. This amounts to clerical oligarchy where lay people have no say in matters of legislation or governance and can have no real or effective participation in the running of the Church.

Where this insertion into the code comes from is not clear; what is clear is that it is now irrevocable unless this recent incorporation into the revised code is rescinded. Priestly anointing is deemed necessary for legitimate exercise of divine power. You either have that power or you don't; if you don't, you can't have any effective participation in government; and the only way to plug into this source of power is through priestly ordination. The logic at least is consistent.

What was the big deal, I asked myself, about 'exercising power' in a small rural community in County Limerick, Ireland? An abbot might be

---

95   Can. 129 §1. Those who have received sacred orders are qualified according to the norms of the prescripts of the law, for the power of governance, which exists in the Church by divine institution and is also called the power of jurisdiction. §2. Lay members of the Christian faithful can cooperate in the exercise of this same power according to the norm of law.

96   I have tried to understand the reasoning of the Catholic Church in its refusal to ordain women as priests in chapter eight of my book *The Opal and the Pearl*, Dublin, Columba Books, 2017, pp. 195-206.

asked to comment upon some issue pertinent to Roman Catholicism and so be expected both to know and to uphold the party line. The danger of some maverick monk leading the faithful astray is somewhat curtailed by his being harnessed to and governed by the norms and regulations pertaining to ordained priesthood.

I did find that I was suddenly expected to make public statements about everything and anything: 'Why was Stephen Ireland playing midfielder for Manchester City and not playing for Trappatoni's Ireland?' 'Is Barack Obama digging us out of the hole — international as well as financial - that he inherited from George Bush or is he digging deeper into it?' At least I understood the language in which such questions were being posed; others were complete gobbledegook: 'Should Google remove Buzz from Gmail?'

Other questions were of huge moral significance but had nothing to do with Roman Catholicism as such: 'Should Shell be allowed to build a pipeline to deliver raw natural gas from the Corrib field to Bellanaboy?' 'Should Dustin the Turkey be allowed to represent Ireland at the Eurovision song contest?' 'Should Angelina Jolie and Brad Pitt reunite?' 'Should Jedward have been eliminated from the X-Factor on 22nd November, 2009?' All these paled to insignificance in the wake of a letter asking the new Abbot of Glenstal to address, as keynote speaker, a 'Charity Investment Conference' in the Westin Hotel, Dublin. I wrote to say that I had joined Glenstal Abbey at twenty years of age, had never signed a cheque in my life until I was fifty-two, and was the last person on the planet qualified to address this meeting. I realised then what it must feel like when, having won something like a Miss World competition, you are asked to comment on the political situation in Nicaragua.

On the feast of the Transfiguration, 6th August, 2013, I get a phone call in the morning to say that the Governor of California, who is staying at the Dunraven Arms in Adare during a visit to Ireland, wishes to hear some Gregorian chant and will be visiting Glenstal Abbey in the early afternoon. Panic manoeuvres all round. What shall we do? Will he have tea? How many are coming? How can we arrange Gregorian chant in mid-afternoon? All hands on deck. We spend the next couple of hours cleaning, scrubbing, cooking, clearing, getting ready to look natural, normal and ordinary when the cavalcade arrives at 2pm.

We all thought it was The Terminator himself, Arnie Schwarzenegger, come to suss out our castle as an ideal setting for his next movie. I mean who ever heard of a Governor of California who wasn't Arnold Schwarzenegger? If you are asked on a Quiz Show: Governor of California? Your automatic response is Arnie Schwarzenegger. Out of the car steps an ordinary dapper human being called Jerry Brown. Governor Jerry Brown of California and his wife, Anne Gust Brown, visiting Europe for two weeks this summer to find relatives and sites connected to their great-grandparents. One of these emigrated from Germany in 1848; another fled from Ireland during the famine. While the trip was largely personal, they met with Eamon Gilmore when they arrived and with Edna Kenny the day before they left. One week in Germany and one week in Ireland doesn't give much time for comprehensive viewing. They met renewable energy experts in Germany, did a tour of an auto plant in Munich and visited the Dachau concentration camp.

His ancestors in Ireland came from Tipperary; they met various cousins while staying in Adare. But on one Wednesday of that one week visit to Ireland they suddenly decide to spend one of their precious afternoons at Glenstal Abbey.

When dealing with someone as high-powered and charismatic as Jerry Brown, what he says and does, especially on a whirlwind tour of his ancestral country, is emblematic. The visit was first of all about himself and his own roots; but it also had to do with Ireland and we would do well to read the symbolism of his time here. One of the secrets to understanding him is his Jesuit education. Not only was he at school with the Jesuits but he became a Jesuit himself for six years before leaving the seminary and becoming Governor of California for the first time from 1975 to 1983. He developed a great affinity with James Joyce, as intense and as tortured an ex-Jesuit student as himself. He quotes verbatim the lines of Joyce at the end of *A Portrait of the Artist as a Young Man*:

> Welcome, O life! I go to encounter for the millionth time the reality of experience and to forge in the smithy of my soul the uncreated conscience of my race.

Joyce had become the short-cut to his own connection with Ireland. He signed the guestbook here: '*ad majora natus sum*' the motto of some Jesuit schools: 'I was born for greater things.'

The detour to a Benedictine monastery in central Ireland was also a commentary on the Ireland of his roots; the Ireland he was encountering on his visit. He had seen the Book of Kells and somehow felt that the secret for Ireland was to retrieve something of the artistry and the selfless artisanal work ethic of those medieval geniuses. Economically Ireland was buffeted by the waves of world market forces and had little control of its fragile future. But deep down in the soul of Ireland there was an artistry and an integrity that, if retrieved, would be 'the uncreated conscience' that would see us right. And so, he wanted to find a place where Latin was understood and Gregorian chant was sung on a daily basis. Was it an intuition similar to that of W.B. Yeats: 'I think if I could be given a month of antiquity and leave to spend it where I chose, I would spend it in Byzantium, a little before Justinian opened St Sophia and closed the Academy of Plato.'

But, the question for me was this: did I need to be an ordained priest to complete any of these assignments. As for celebrating the sacraments and the Eucharist, there were over twenty other ordained priests in the community at Glenstal who could preside in that way.

Dear Santa

Heading for Waterford from Dublin in February 2010, I passed by Jerpoint Abbey which triggered a memory that St Nicholas was meant to have been buried there. The Normans, who left so many souvenirs in our own County Limerick, began their invasion of Ireland in 1169 at the request of the ousted king of Leinster, Dermot McMurrough. Two years later Henry II landed an army in Waterford to establish control over the people of Ireland and, more importantly, over the unruly force that had gone before him. John, the youngest of five sons of King Henry, nicknamed 'Lackland' because he didn't have any of his own, became Lord of Ireland in 1177. His visit to Limerick left us King John's castle, more a monument to his unpopularity and need to protect himself than to any outstanding architectural originality. It was completed around the year 1200. Limerick prospered under the Normans, becoming a busy port and trading centre, but it had to be divided into two areas as a result: 'English Town' on King's Island and 'Irish Town' on the south bank of the river.

One of the ways the Normans kept the natives under control was to establish monasteries which would organise and regulate the surrounding countryside. The Cistercian Jerpoint Abbey was founded in 1183. To persuade the local population of the monastery's divine approval, it was important to have buried there the relics of some saint of high standing with a guaranteed reputation for miracle working. St Nicholas, whose moniker was 'the wonderworker' ticked all the boxes. He had lived in Myra, present day Turkey, from around 270 until he died on 6th December, 343. Myra was another name for the older metropolis of Lycia which is associated with Saint Paul's having changed ships in its harbour on one occasion. The earliest church of St Nicholas at Myra, in the place where the saint was buried, dates from the sixth century. The present-day church was constructed mainly from the eighth century onward. From the beginning of the ninth century, Myra was overtaken by Muslims. After a siege in 809, the town fell to Harun al Raschid and later in the eleventh century it was again overrun by Islamic invaders.

During these times of oppression the plunder of St Nicholas' grave began. Taking advantage of wartime confusion, sailors from Bari in 1087 collected half of Nicholas' skeleton, leaving the rest in his grave. This first portion of relics (about half of the bones) were translated to Bari, where they still are housed in the church of St Stephen. The remainder was later removed by Venetians during the First Crusade (1096–1099) and taken to Venice in 1100. Scientific investigation has established that the relics in Bari and in Venice belong to the same skeleton, whether that be St Nicholas or not has yet to be confirmed.

The Irish version of the story tells of a Norman family, the de Frainets (or Frenet) who owned properties in Thomastown, Co. Kilkenny. One of these, while on crusade to the Holy Land, helped to transport the relics of Saint Nicholas from Myra to Bari while Bari was under Norman rule. When the Normans were forced out of Italy, the family moved at first to Nice in France, and when the Normans lost their hegemony in France, moved to Ireland. This de Frenet would then have brought some of the relics of Saint Nicholas to be buried in Jerpoint around the year 1200.

I arrived at Jerpoint Abbey in 2010. I asked the two women at the interpretative centre where Santa Claus was buried. They said – he is not here but he is in Old Town Jerpoint a few miles away. 'First turn right after the Abbey on the way towards Waterford. The graveyard is on private lands but the owner will let you in if you tell him we sent you.' I could not find the place at first but arrived at a B&B called Old Town Farmhouse and asked the lady of the house where Santa Claus was buried. She said 'We're all Normans here!' Her name was Fitzgerald. They had all heard this rumour but thought it was a myth. She told me to drive past the entrance to Mount Juliet and there I would find on the left a gateway to Old Town where a graveyard was situated. The farm was called Belmore House. I rang the intercom at the gate and a voice told me to enter the avenue, take the first field road on the right, and walk over that field to the ruined church and graveyard. I did this and found a beautiful little ruined church with a graveyard overlooking Jerpoint Abbey. One large broken grave stone slab showed three barely discernible carved figures, one of whom appeared to be St Nicholas. The others were said to be the two crusaders who brought him there. The church dates from 1170, the grave slab from the 1300s.

This church of St Nicholas is all that remains of the medieval village, Newtown Jerpoint, that fell to ruin in the seventeenth century. The village had at one time surrounded the Cistercian Jerpoint Abbey, but must have become derelict after the suppression of the monasteries by Henry VIII in 1540.

So who is St Nicholas – and what did he ever do for Ireland? Nicholas is patron saint of sailors, stockbrokers, pawn-brokers, children and young women who are looking for a husband and who don't have a dowry sufficient to get married. In Myra his house was beside three others where the daughters had come to marriageable age but could not get a husband because they didn't have a dowry. Nicholas took three bags of gold and threw one through the front door of the first house, one through the front door of the second house, and because the front door of the third house was closed he climbed up onto the roof and lowered the bag of gold down the chimney. These three bags of gold are the round symbols still to be seen outside the doors of many a pawn-broker shop. When Dutch settlers founded New York (New Amsterdam) they brought St Nicholas with them as their patron. They called him *Sinta* [Nic] *Claus* which is why he has returned to us in modern dress as Santa Claus.

So, why would Santa Claus, Saint Nicholas, want to have his remains resurrected in Ireland at this time? Let us imagine him now as patron saint of the great train robbery we are hoping to effect, a kind of medieval Ronnie Biggs. His name means 'Nico' which is 'triumph' in Greek, and 'laos' which means 'people,' from which our word 'laity' derives. Put together Nicolaus stands for 'triumph of the laity'. Nicholas the wonderworker and patron of the laity will help us to take back the Church of Jesus Christ to and for ourselves.

Pray, Pay and Obey

When we talk about the 'triumph of the laity', we have to admit that over the 2,000 year history of the Church as an institution, the so-called laity have had limited profile. In a hierarchical feudal world, ordinary people never counted for much. From the earliest times an option was taken for those who lived the so-called 'religious' life over and above those who supposedly 'lived in the world'. Celibacy was lauded and sexuality deplored. Marriage was tolerated as necessary to keep the population going, but married couples were way down the list on the ladder of perfection.

Another useful member of our hold-up team is John Henry Newman (1801–1890). He lived through most of the nineteenth century, was beatified on 19th December, 2010, by Pope Benedict XVI and canonised by Pope Francis on 13th October, 2019. Newman was a convert to Roman Catholicism as from 1845. Originally, he had been an evangelical Oxford clergyman of the Church of England. He ranks among Christianity's greatest thinkers and has already been proposed as a Doctor of the Church. From very early in his career within the Catholic Church he fell foul of conservative authorities because he wanted to hold consultations with lay people.

He published in a review called the *Rambler* in July, 1859 an article *On Consulting the Faithful in Matters of Doctrine*, which, at the time was tantamount to - and I quote from an authoritative source - 'an act of political suicide from which his career within the Church was never fully to recover; at one stroke he, whose reputation as the one honest broker between the extremes of English Catholic opinion had hitherto stood untarnished, gained the Pope's personal displeasure, the reputation at Rome of being the most dangerous man in England, and a formal accusation of heresy proffered against him by the Bishop of Newport.'[97] And all this because he was proposing that the laity should be consulted by bishops.

'What is the province of the laity? To hunt, to shoot, to entertain,' wrote Monsignor George Talbot in protest against Newman. 'If a check not be placed on the laity in England they will be the rulers of the Catholic Church instead of the Holy See and the Episcopate.' Bishop Ullathorne,

....

97 John Henry Newman, *On Consulting the Faithful in Matters of Doctrine*, with an Introduction by John Coulson, London 1961: reissued with a Foreword by Derek Worlock. Archbishop of Liverpool, London, 1986, p. 2.

Newman's Ordinary, asked, 'Who are the laity?' And as Newman noted, 'I answered (not in these words) that the Church would look [somewhat] foolish without them.'[98]

As we move into the second decade of the twenty-first century, things have changed dramatically. Democracy is the idiom of most civilised countries, and educated people are not just used to having their voices heard, but they regard it as their basic right to have a say in all important matters which concern their well-being. We have to remind ourselves, therefore, in the aftermath of a particularly unfriendly history where the laity are concerned in the Catholic Church, that our tradition has always carried a train of theological thought (although discreetly hidden, we would have to say) very much in their favour.

In Roman Catholic tradition, the *sensus fidelium* or the 'consensus among the faithful', is the idea that beliefs of 'ordinary' Catholics are one of the valid sources of truth in Catholic theology. This is something which religious leaders are supposed to consult when making decisions about Catholic doctrine. The *sensus fidelium* was even regarded by Newman as one way of discovering the true tradition of the Church. 'Sometimes by the mouth of the episcopacy, sometimes by the doctors, sometimes by the people,' Newman wrote in his article in *The Rambler*, 'sometimes by liturgies, rites, ceremonies, and customs, by events, disputes, movements, and all those other phenomena which are comprised under the name of history.'[99] These words were written ten years before the definition of papal infallibility. It should not be forgotten that 'infallibility' is the charism of the whole Church and there are manifestations of it other than the very specific role of the Pope. Pope Benedict XVI said during an impromptu address to priests in Aosta in July 2005: 'The Pope is not an oracle; he is infallible in very rare situations, as we know.'

The teaching of the Church regarding the infallibility of the faithful was never lost even though it had been ignored since the Council of

98   Ibid p. 18-19.
99   John Henry Newman, 'On Consulting the Faithful', *The Rambler*, July, 1859.

Trent. Vatican II reasserted it saying that 'the entire body of the faithful ... cannot err in matters of belief. They manifest this special property ... when they show universal agreement in matters of faith and morals.'[100]

Never before in the history of the Church has the absolutely essential role of the layperson been so emphatically needed as now. Vatican II called for a renewal in the life and role of the laity. Yet there still seems to be a fundamental lack of understanding of the lay vocation and its role in the Church's mission. For many, there is a notion that the only real vocation in the Church is the ordained priesthood. But in fact, the actual teaching of the Church is that laypeople have a distinct and very real role in the spreading of the Gospel, which the Church desperately needs them to carry out with the authority, creativity and power that the Holy Spirit has given them in Baptism. Everyone receives the Holy Spirit in Baptism; this makes everyone a priest and a prophet, and there is nothing 'higher' or nothing 'more' that can be given or received than this gift of the Person of the Holy Spirit, which makes every single one of us equal and unique.

One of the burning issues at Vatican II became known as 'collegiality'. This was essentially a question of the relationship which should pertain between bishops and the pope. 'What kind of authority did the bishops have over the Church at large when they acted collectively, that is, collegially; how was that authority exercised in relationship to the pope; and how was collegiality different from 'Conciliarism' (supremacy of a council over the pope), a position condemned in the fifteenth century and repeatedly condemned thereafter?

Collegiality became a lightning-rod issue. It galvanised the centripetal tendencies into full collision with the centrifugal. The first group condemned it as 'unworkable, unacceptable, dangerous, even 'heretical'. Conciliarism and Gallicanism had both been condemned by popes.

---

100 *Lumen Gentium*, Art. 12.

Conservatives put collegiality into these same categories and regarded it as incompatible with papal primacy. The progressive group on the other hand regarded collegiality as the linchpin of the centre-periphery relationship. Bishops, they said, are not branch managers of local offices of the Holy See.[101]

The end of a 'clerical' priesthood

Decluttering can never be enough; a far more radical defenestration is required. The need for a declericisation of Catholicism should not be too surprising to us today, says Fr Gerry O'Hanlon. The harrowing history of abuse for which there has to be at some point a complete 'reckoning; the theological interrogation of priesthood in the light of the rediscovery of the dignity of the lay vocation, and now the insistence by Pope Francis that priests are called to servant-leadership all mean that a whole way of life has been called into question. For a priest today it seems clear that 'come follow me' requires the end of clericalism: and the invitation of the Lord is addressed to each of us – what do you want? Do you want to engage in this project for Church renewal?

'In travelling around Ireland meeting and talking with groups of priests, the odd bishop and laity it is striking how often lay people say: "they just won't let go." They are speaking of me and you, we priests!'[102]

The very word 'clerical' in English has a double meaning which suggests also literacy and administrative competence. The clergy were an aristocracy set apart from the lower ranks of Church membership. When we hear both lawyers and doctors referring to those outside their particular competences as 'lay' people, we begin to understand the hiatus between 'clerical' and 'lay' which derived from the Roman Empire. The university gown (the distinction between gown and town) is yet another

---

101 John W. O'Malley, *What Happened at Vatican II*, The Belknap Press of Harvard University Press, Cambridge, Massachusetts, 2008.

102 Gerry O'Hanlon, 'Church and State in a Changing Environment,' *The Furrow*, September, 2019, p. 505.

long robe distinguishing the dignitary from the great unwashed and advertising the wearer as 'a cleric'.

The Protestant Reformation was to no small degree a reaction against the clericalism of the Middle Ages. The Council of Trent in counter-reaction decisively affirmed the distinction between the ministerial priesthood and the priesthood of the faithful. A strongly sacerdotalist approach to ministry became a hallmark of Catholicism against Protestantism. They had ministers who were married, who 'took the service' and preached; we had priests who were celibate, who offered the sacrifice of the Mass, and were the real deal.

Chapter Three of *Lumen Gentium*, the document of the Second Vatican Council, deals with Church hierarchy and has a whole later Chapter Four on the vocation of the laity. Cardinal Manning had proclaimed that 'There can be conceived no office higher, and no power greater than the office of the priest'; Vatican II seemed to puncture definitively the tyres of this sacerdotomobile.

Authority in the Church of Jesus Christ should have only one role: to establish a household where the life and love of the three persons of the Trinity become the cornerstone. From what Jesus Christ has revealed, and the Holy Spirit has taught, this life of the Trinity is a mystery of love between persons, where no one lords it over anyone else, where no one is 'superior' to anyone else, where the one in charge is the servant of all. Every person in authority in the Church should make it their daily concern to find out whether our institutions, our traditions, our rules, our rituals, our administrative practices, are promoting this community's existence as persons in communion. If they are facilitating in any way prejudice, intolerance, elitism, discrimination, competition, domination or alienation, they should be altered or removed. We may have turned the household of God into a House of Lords or a Game of Thrones. God has to be allowed to overturn and transform any social, political, racial and psychological structures which have been put in place to gain control and exercise arbitrary authority over others. The Church should be a transparent and radiant icon of the Trinity in our midst. The Trinity is the revelation to us of the true meaning of the word 'person' and the true meaning of whatever we call 'love'. Of its nature it requires the elimination of whatever might reduce us to the pre-personal, the impersonal the anti-personal.

Michael Francis Sadlier (1925-1999)

One of the curates in Granagh/Ballingarry when I was a child was Michael Francis Sadlier. He wrote a memoir at the end of his life which he called 'Brainwashed from Birth'.[103] It begins: 'If I knew what was being done to me the day I was baptised a traditional Catholic, I would certainly have shouted stop.' He was born in Limerick in 1925. Chapter Two of his memoir is called 'Choosing a Career with Misguidance'.

> Traditional Catholicism was full of false formulae. A priest at ordination was said to receive extra powers to be a man of God over and above those given to lay Catholics at their Baptism and Confirmation.

Inviting lay people to read the word of God in the new Mass, his parish priest admitted: 'It won't be hard for ye to do it better than the curate and myself. And that isn't praising ye either.'

> Apart from the breviary which they read mechanically, and the daily Mass for which they got a stipend, many priests said far less prayers than many of their parishioners ... The extra powers given at ordination can only have been magical ones for consecrating the Eucharist and administering the sacraments. The clerical closed-shop was the only thing that prevented giving such powers to all Catholics, women as well as men.

....

103 Unpublished memoir shown to me by Michael's niece, Julie Sadlier, with permission to publish these extracts.

In September 1942 Michael Sadlier 'left home in the black suit of the cleric, to cut myself off from the world and its joys for love of Christ and all the souls I innocently believed would never be saved if I didn't do so'. He was ordained a priest and after a year teaching at St Munchin's College, was appointed curate to the parish of Ballingarry with residence at Granagh. My mother thought his sermons were the best she had ever heard. He was certainly a great adornment to Granagh, which regarded itself as a completely separate entity, never using the extended title of Granagh/Ballingarry. He was equally complimentary about us:

> Granagh was a completely rural parish. Country life was nothing new to me, half reared as I had been in Caherconlish. But Caherconlish was a village. You could never escape the sensation of being surrounded by people. It was houses with fields around them. Granagh was fields with houses inside them.
>
> Culturally too Granagh was something I had never before experienced. Maybe it was because I found myself regarded as its leader that I was so community-consious there. Maybe it helped that being considered an outsider, a city man among the farmers, I could stand back far enough from rural routine to see in action a community more self-conscious and less class-conscious than I could hitherto visualise ... It was the nearest I ever came to seeing a Christian community approximate to the ideal. And my predecessors agreed with this opinion.

The church at Granagh was directly in front of Knockfierna and Chapter Eight of his memoir is called 'The Hill of Truth'.

> I had heard of it when leprechauns were seen there and people went out from Limerick city to catch some. It stood in the centre of the parish, a landmark visible for miles around. I crossed over its shoulder on my way to Ballingarry, until one of the roads in the plain was tarred and I could make better time going round it ...

The list of townslands was read out in church three times a year with the names of residents who had paid their Christmas, Easter and Lenten dues. Priests might enliven this somewhat mercenary recital with a running commentary. Where a Protestant might have bought Catholic land but had continued to pay the dues on it, a priest of the locality was recorded as saying: 'Paddy O'Donnell, Kilduff, ten shillings, Reginald Rothman, Ballyruss, a Protestant, ten pounds. 'I wish to God ye were all Protestants!'

The final chapter of Michael Sadlier's memoir is called 'On Leaving Everything to Follow Christ'.

> I never thought I'd see the day that conscience would compel me to leave the traditional Catholic Church to follow Christ in accordance with the gospels. This seemed absolutely impossible thirty years ago when I was misled into leaving everything to follow him in accordance with the Code of Canon Law. I had nothing to leave then but the uncertainties of adolescence. After seven years imprisonment in Maynooth I could return to Limerick and live happily ever after in imposing parish houses with plenty of pocket money and little to do.
>
> It was customary on Holy Thursday to spend some time before the 'altar of repose' thinking especially about Christ's agony in the garden and his rebuke to the disciples, 'Could you not watch one hour with me?' It was a time when you thought a lot about the purpose of a paid professional priesthood and its ever-increasing irrelevancy.
>
> It was on Holy Thursday of 1971 that I finally decided to abandon traditional Catholicism ... Nothing could excuse our refusal to admit that the traditional concept of the priesthood would have to be drastically revised if not abandoned. It cannot coexist with the new 'people of God' idea nor with the methods now available for spreading the Good News.

Fr Tony Coote (1964–2019)

He came to Glenstal Abbey twice before he died in 2019. You got the impression he was aware that he was not simply dying his own death, but in some strangely prophetic way, was being asked to die the symbolic death of a whole kind of priesthood.

Fr Tony Coote, aged 56, (1964–2019) was a priest based in the Mount Merrion and Kilmacud parishes in south county Dublin. He was shocked in February, 2018 to find himself diagnosed with motor neuron disease (MND). Motor Neuron Disease is incurable and affects nerve cells that send messages to the brain causing a progressive weakening of all the muscles in the body. In November of 2017 he had an unusual fall which gave him problems with his left hand. An MRI scan established that he had MND and since then his health began to deteriorate rapidly. He went public on all this and wrote his autobiography, *Live While You Can: A Memoir of Faith, Hope and the Power of Acceptance*,[104] which was launched in May, 2019.

Five months after the diagnosis, he decided to show himself to the whole country and display the condition he was in. Under the banner 'Walk While You Can', he set off on a mountain trike - as he was unable to walk - from Letterkenny, Co. Donegal on Monday, 6th August, 2018, the Feast of the Transfiguration, to undertake a 550km journey to Ballydehob in Co. Cork. With a target of €250,000, he raised €700,000 to aid research into the condition, about which relatively little was known, and for the care of those living with the illness. He died a year later on 28th August, 2019. 'I'm not a hero,' he says 'I'm simply someone living with a condition that has challenged me to live another way, and given me an opportunity to experience life as almost helpless, relying on the assistance of others.'

MND could read 'Melchisedek Now Dies' and Tony could be seen as a prophetic mimeograph of the demise of priesthood as we have known it. He tells in his memoir of his own eventual acceptance of this disintegration.

....

104 Tony Coote, *Live While You Can: A Memoir of Faith, Hope and the Power of Acceptance*, Dublin, Hachette Books, Ireland, 2019.

He remembers the great feeling of vulnerability he experienced early on during his illness. He had been a carer all his life and now the roles were reversed. He had to allow himself to be cared for. He knew from the beginning that the people around him were only too anxious to be of service, to help him in any way, but this willingness only increased his embarrassment. He had to learn how to be at the receiving end of other people's ministrations. He eventually had to give in and allow others to intervene since he was unable even to tie his own shoe laces.

The Dublin parishes where he worked provided an interesting reversal of previous norms. The relatively consistent congregations were mainly middle class people whose faith was deeply rooted. In the past, such diligence had been the prerogative of the poor. As a result, many had already taken over responsibility for areas such as finance, communications, arrangement of liturgies, etc. It only remained for them to help Tony Coote in every way to celebrate Mass at a small table in front of the main altar when he could no longer even hold a fork or a spoon in his hand.

Tony Coote teaches us how the priesthood we have known is asked to let go and to prepare the people to take over and to assume their own very real but dormant role as priests.

Priests come from the people, remain with the people, are at the service of the people. What need is there for such servants to be removed from their natural environment to receive preparation in isolation for their return to service among those same people. What need for them to be placed in 'seminaries' as if they were the Dalai Lama or some protected species which needed specialised breeding facilities to safeguard against worldly contamination.

David Phillip Vetter, a boy from Texas, was born with a genetic disease known as 'severe combined immune deficiency syndrome' (SCID). This required him to live almost his entire life in a sterilised, bubble-shaped cocoon at the Texas Children's Hospital in Houston, to 'isolate' him from germs and viruses. His condition made him famous in the media, where he was known as 'the boy in the plastic bubble'. David died on February 22, 1984 at the age of twelve. The bubble-shaped isolation unit in which he lived, created by NASA at the Johnson Space Centre, can be seen at the Smithsonian's National Museum of American History. Vetter's tragic life and death brought up many ethical issues about the viability of such 'isolation' treatment. Might not David's life be a vivid image of conditions we have imposed on Catholic priesthood in the past?

'Just as we call all Christians "Christ" in virtue of their anointing, so we call them all "priests" [sacerdotes] because they are all members of the one Priest. The apostle Peter therefore says of them that they are "a holy people, a royal priesthood". Clearly this does not refer only to the bishops and presbyters who are now distinguished by the name of "priests" in the Church.'[105] This is St Augustine writing about *The City of God* in the fourth century.

One of the most significant roles for the ministerial priesthood in today's Roman Catholic Church might be to educate the community to an understanding and living expression of their own priesthood. Pope John Paul II reminded us that the role and task of the ordained minister is to 'promote the baptismal priesthood of the entire people of God, leading it to its full ecclesial realisation.'[106] The ministerial priesthood 'is directed to the unfolding of the baptismal grace of all Christians'.[107]

....

105 Augustine, *The City of God Against the Pagans*, Bk XX, Chapter 10.
106 Apostolic Exhortation, *Pastores Dabo Vobis*, n.17.
107 *Catechism of the Catholic Church*, n. 1547.

X

'Alive with what's invisible'

Seamus Heaney, who was born five years before I was, has this to say about our generation:

> I believe that the condition into which I was born and into which my generation in Ireland was born involved the moment of transition from sacred to profane. Other peoples, other cultures, had to go through it earlier – the transition from a condition where your space, the space of the world, had a determined meaning and a sacred possibility, to a condition where space was a neuter geometrical disposition without any emotional or inherited meaning.[108]

Heaney would try to 'forge' a connection between the world we experience around us and another world which he would have been brought up to call 'supernatural'. He would reject the presentation of such a world which his religion and his culture outlined as a dogmatic belief structure, and would meticulously explore and redefine in his own words the possibility of such connection as he experienced it personally and poetically. His official religion and his literary vocation were at odds in this domain, and one of his tasks was to come to terms with such antagonism.[109]

....

108 Interview with Seamus Heaney by Randy Brandes, Salmagundi, 80, 6 (quoted in Daniel Tobin, *Passage to the Center*, University Press of Kentucky, 1999, p. 5.).

109 'I was wanting to write about contemporary Ireland, the Republic of Ireland, as a country with a religious subconscious but a secular destiny - at the point of transition from the communality of religious devotion to the loneliness of modernity and subjectivity. The community in the poem has lost the sense of its own destiny and of any metaphysical call.' Here Heaney is talking about his poem, 'The Mud Vision' from the collection *The Haw Lantern* (1987) [cf. *Opened Ground, Poems 1966-1996*, London, Faber, 1998, p. 321] in the 1997 interview, The Art of Poetry, No 75, *The Paris Review*, No 144, Fall 1997.

The metaphysics to which Heaney's poetry introduces us is not 'beyond' (as the word 'meta' means in Greek) the physical world in which we live; it is a dimension of that very world itself. Nor is it 'above' the natural world as words like 'supernatural' might imply. It may not be readily visible to us who live so avidly and one-dimensionally in its turmoil, but that does not mean that it does not exist and is situated squarely within it. There is certainly another reality but it is within this one in which we live. Heaney introduces us to a 'double vision,' which detects in the visible world traces of the invisible. Our role, in this hologrammatic countryside should be to welcome others and introduce them to this binocular possibility, available to even the most skeptical tourist, if shown the way. The crock of gold beneath every crimson rainbow was under my feet all the time. To achieve this optic we must close down our 'normal' 'ordinary' 'commonsense' way of viewing the world around us, and provide ourselves with the 3D goggles, as it were, which can supply a depth charge of unfathomableness to every familiarity. Everything we see around us has this extra dimension, is alive with the invisible; we have to attune ourselves to detecting this hidden layer.[110]

Heaney undertook such an archaeological dig on behalf of humanity. He developed an alphabet and a vocabulary to help us adapt to 'being in depth'. In one kind of survey map all that is required is topographical depiction: representation of an area of land or sea showing physical features. In this other kind of vision and representation, someone's heart has to provide an alternative compass. Heaney's poetry introduces us to such 'heartwork'. Particular realities in our world are naturally 'sacramental', they can act as portals to the unknown, windows on the invisible.

Looking at water carved in stone on a cathedral façade, Heaney sees a hidden world conjured by the sculptor's art. A block of stone carries a secret message where an artist has chiseled significant grooves representing water onto the surface. Stone provides durability; art inscribes subtlety.

....

110 A more formal and extended treatment of this can be found in my book *Living the Mystery*, Dublin, Columba Books, 2019.

'What we find, then, at the root of Heaney's poetry is a conjunction of the sources of art and religion.'[111] Heaney writes hieroglyphs which give access to hiddenness. Open Sesame.

Ireland is its own island. As such it is self-contained and does not need anything or anywhere else to fulfil its deepest dimensions. People who have lived on this island have left detectable grooves on the surface, footprints from pathfinders. Natural forces, wind and weather, storm and sea, have changed the physical features and sculpted designs for us to read. We who stand on this same surface many years later can find in this same reality both the original contours, the birthmarks and the scripts that have been scratched into the visitors' book. One set comes as 'scripture', the other as 'nature'. Both can be used to elaborate our own stance at this time.

The Equine Archetype

Crimson and Gold describes a childhood in County Limerick which, by mid-twentieth century, was a Protestant enclave in a Catholic country. Horses were the common denominator. But horses cannot be held responsible for anything. Animals are determined by nature. They do nothing more than instinctively fulfil the pattern inscribed in their genes and chromosomes. They are DNA docile. We, on the other hand, are perfectly capable of changing our patterns of behaviour. What is called the 'constructionist view' of evolution suggests that we are not only capable of changing ourselves and our culture but we are biologically built to do so. Far from being predetermined either by our environment or our genes, we are provided with an adaptive plasticity which awaits our decisive action before it forms us into the eventual shape we choose to become. We are not hardwired by our hormones to any form of behaviour.

Horses evolved sixty million years ago as *Eohippus*, a four-toed, leaf-eating forest dweller with the profile of a medium-sized dog. Today's

111 Daniel Tobin, *Passage to the Center*, University Press of Kentucky, 1999, p. 4.

horse, *Equus Caballus*, has been around for 20 million years. Late Palaeolithic humans hunted wild horses for food, used them in ritual, and depicted them in cave art all over Europe. As an herbivore, a horse preys on no other animal, but is itself the target of predators such as large cats and wolf packs. Most horses take flight under stress, but when domesticated for farm work or for battle, a horse has been known for bravery, aggression and selflessness. In other words, any belligerence or bloodthirstiness in horses is our doing, not theirs.

Alexander the Great, king and conqueror of antiquity, was a skilled horseman. Bucephalus, his horse, is almost as legendary as himself. According to Plutarch, thirteen-year-old Alexander tamed the horse when no one else could do so, by turning it away from its own shadow. Bucephalus was afraid of his shadow. Freed from this fear, the wild horse became a legend. Some told of his descent from Greek gods, others prophesied that whoever rode Bucephalus would rule the world. Some held that the horse was born on the same day as the king; others that they died simultaneously. In fact, Alexander outlived his horse and named the city of Bucephala, in his honour.

Napoleon's horse Marengo, who fought with the emperor at the battle of Waterloo, was so famous that he is still on display at the National Army Museum in London, after painstaking restoration and remounting of his skeleton.

The most trusted advisor of the Roman emperor, Caligula, was a horse. According to Suetonius, Incitatus (meaning 'swift' or 'at full gallop') had a stable made of marble and a stall made of ivory. He wore only purple blankets, the colour of royalty, and had jewels hanging from his neck. The horse had his own private servants who supplied him with oats mixed with gold flakes. On his birthday, the emperor would issue invitations to lavish birthday parties on the horse's behalf. It is said that Caligula planned to make Incitatus a Consul, that is, one of the two chief magistrates of the Roman Republic.

And where would Roy Rogers be without Trigger (1934-1965)? Originally named Golden Cloud, he was a palomino born in San Diego,

California. When Roy was preparing to make his first movie in a starring role, he was offered a choice of five rented 'movie' horses but he chose Golden Cloud. Rogers bought him eventually in 1943 and renamed him Trigger for his deftness of hoof and head. Trigger learned 150 tricks and could walk 50 feet on his hind legs. He was able to sit in a chair, sign his name 'X' with a pencil, lie down for a nap and cover himself with a blanket. Rogers also managed to get Trigger housetrained. 'Spending as much time as he does in hotels, theatres and hospitals, this ability comes in might handy,' Rogers said. This feat was regarded by most trainers of horses as Trigger's greatest accomplishment. No need for 'Cappa Magna' for Trigger or for Roy.

Humans are responsible for all these so-called accomplishments. No horse would ever have gone hunting with the Limericks of its own free will, unless carefully tutored by members of that hunt.

Fox hunting with hounds, as a formalised activity, began in England in the sixteenth century, in a form very similar to that practised today.

A traditional fox hunt starts with hounds being 'cast' or put into rough, overgrown, areas called 'coverts', where foxes hide during daylight hours. If the hounds pick up the scent of a fox, they start to track it, and the horse riders follow by the most direct route possible. This involves skilled, energetic and athletic horse riding, which makes it easy to see why fox hunting was the background to equestrian sports such as steeplechase and point-to-point racing. The hunt for the fox continues until either the animal escapes, goes to ground (hides in an underground burrow or den) or is caught and usually killed by the hounds. If the fox goes to ground, terriers are sometimes sent into the burrow to locate the fox so that it can be dug out and killed.

Roald Dahl tells the story from the other point of view in his children's novel *Magnificent Mr Fox* (1979). Mr Fox is an anthropomorphic, tricky and cunning individual who lives underground beside a tree with his wife and four children. In order to feed his family, he makes nightly visits to farms owned by three nasty, dim-witted farmers Boggis, Bunce and Bean. Tired of being outsmarted by Mr Fox, the triumvirate devise a plan to ambush him as he leaves his burrow, but they succeed only in shooting off his tail.

The three then dig up the Foxes' burrow using spades and excavators. The Foxes manage to escape by burrowing further beneath the earth to safety. The trio outside are ridiculed for their persistence but they refuse to give up and vow not to return to their farms until they have caught Mr Fox. They lay siege and wait until Mr Fox is hungry enough to come out. Cornered by their enemies, Mr Fox and his family, and all the other underground creatures that live around the hill, begin to starve.

After three days trapped underground, Mr Fox devises a plot to acquire food. Working from his memory of the routes he has taken above ground, he and his children tunnel through the ground and wind up burrowing to one of four chicken houses. Mr Fox kills several chickens and sends his eldest son to carry the animals back home to Mrs Fox. On the way to their next destination, Mr Fox runs into his friend Badger and asks him to accompany him on his mission, as well as to extend an invitation to the feast to the other burrowing animals - Badger and his family, as well as the Moles, the Rabbits and the Weasels. Aided by Badger, the animals tunnel to Bunce's storehouse for ducks, geese, hams, bacon and carrots (as noted by one of the Small Foxes, the Rabbits will require vegetables) and then to Bean's secret cider cellar. They carry their loot back home, where Mrs. Fox has prepared a great celebratory banquet for the starving underground animals and their families.

At the table, Mr Fox invites everyone to live in a secret underground neighbourhood with him and his family, where he will hunt for them daily and where none of them will need to worry about the farmers any more. Everyone cheers for this idea, while Boggis, Bunce and Bean are left waiting in vain for the fox to emerge from his den. The book ends with 'And so far as I know, they are *still* waiting'.

Arguments abound for and against fox hunting. Proponents view it as an important part of rural culture, useful for conservation and pest control; opponents see it as cruel and unnecessary. Hunting may have played an important role, next to plant gathering and scavenging, for human survival in prehistoric times, but the vast majority of modern hunters in developed countries stalk and kill animals for recreation. Hunting is a violent and cowardly form of outdoor entertainment, the opposition holds. Thousands of animals are killed each year, many of whom are wounded and die a slow and painful death.

Hunting was banned in Scotland in 2002 and in England and Wales in 2004. There was considerable opposition to the ban; half a million people marched in its support. Many saw it as one further element of the mutual antagonism between town and country, urban and rural dwellers; others situated it in in a lingering class warfare.

It certainly became a political issue in England between Conservative and Labour governments. Perhaps, one of the main reasons why many stalwarts of the Limerick hunt left England in the 1940s was anticipation of the victory of Clement Atlee's Labour party in 1945. Tony Blair wrote in his memoirs, published in 2010, that the Hunting Act of 2004 was 'one of the domestic legislative measures I most regret'. Prime Minister David Cameron stated on 3rd March, 2015 that he planned a free vote in the House of Commons because, 'The Hunting Act has done nothing for animal welfare'. Theresa May expressed her support for a free vote on repealing the ban during the 2017 General Election campaign: 'As it happens, personally, I've always been in favour of fox hunting and we maintain our commitment - we had a commitment previously - as a Conservative Party to allow a free vote and that would allow Parliament to take a decision on this.' Boris Johnston, writing in 2005 in *The Spectator,* which he was editing at the time while also a Conservative MP, described the ban as a Labour government attack on the upper classes. He recommended hunting to all his readers, for 'the "military-style pleasure" of moving as a unit' combined with the 'semi-sexual relation with the horse'.

Fox hunting has never been banned in Ireland, although the lobby is constant and numbers supporting such a ban are considerable. It is difficult to defend what Oscar Wilde has called 'the unspeakable in pursuit of the uneatable', unless you have experienced personally the thrill of the hunt. Town dwellers who have no background in rural activity, find fox hunting barbaric. Arguments about 'pest control' where the fox has no predator above itself on nature's food chain, and therefore needs to be prevented from doing serious damage to farmyards and chicken coops, hardly wash with those who see fox hunting as a blood-thirsty exercise, akin to bull fighting and bear-baiting, designed to accommodate the decadent entertainments of the wealthy.

Well-meaning third-party mediators believed they had found a compromise solution, satisfactory to both sides: the 'drag hunt'. The primary difference between fox hunting and drag hunting is that the hounds are trained to hunt a prepared scent trail laid by someone dragging a material soaked in aniseed or another strong smelling substance. Following a predetermined route over jumps and obstacles, the organisers can avoid no-go areas and tailor the trajectory to suit the riding abilities of the field. The scent, or line, is laid about half an hour before the hunt begins.

Such anodyne alternatives were sneered at by the connoisseurs. Gimmicks for the gormless, this ranked with soft-ball cricket and non-alcoholic beverages: le Marquis without de Sade. Nowadays, despite the ban, many hunts in southern England, according to a new breed of active and articulate hunt saboteurs, pretend to follow a drag, but continue to engage in 'mass murder', and, furthermore, the protesters swear, 'the police are turning a blind eye'. The argument from both sides is as old as the activity itself. Hunters and anti-hunters have stalked each other through parliament, in the press, and in the field, until their antagonism becomes as traditional as the sport itself.

But the horse remains uncontaminated by any such considerations. Horses only do what we train them to do and in recent years their profile has become mightily reduced. For contemporary cultures no longer dependent on horses for food, for draft, or for transportation, the living horse has ceased to be a part of daily experience. Try as we might to find uses for the horse in the twenty-first century, their employment possibilities diminish daily. Thorough-bred race horses trained like athletes have a very short career on the track. What can they do once their short life as champions comes to an end?

Flan O'Brien, whose pen-name Myles na gCopaleen means 'Myles of the little horses', once took up a remark he heard Liam Cosgrave make in the Dáil in respect of racing. Cosgrave had said that he 'looked forward to the day when Irish horses would once again be ambassadors of this country'. Myles took up the idea and ruminated:

> It is no honour to you Irish that you have ... sent away to the ends of the earth perfectly decent, well-bred Irishmen, who never asked for aught save the privilege of sitting in a housheen saturated with soft Irish rain, and being occupied with the wholesome rituals that involve bacon and cabbage, a dish of crubeens, a game of solo and 'kaley tea', by which latter term I allude to your not-easily-surpassed fusion of tannin and potheen. Unhappy men!
>
> Enough! Signs are not wanting that that day is past, never - I pray - to return. A responsible public man has pointed the way. For the future (and, I suppose, subject to the *agrément* of the accepting Power) your representatives abroad are to be horses. It is a delightful remedy, as Irish as Muckish. *The Irish horse is the finest in the world!* He is handsome, his coat is glossy (which is more than can be said about certain non-horse representatives) and he is, by his irrevocable endowments of dignity incapable of vulgar conduct. He is strong, his back is broad. Your old-time Paris diplomat would go to Longchamps and disgrace his office by the pettiness of his bets. Whereas the new Minister can go there, make his way to the starting gate and show the effete exotic bloodstocks of the earth how to look like a horse, run like a hare and be back at the official job the same evening *completely sober!*

It will mean changes, of course, in the subordinate personnel of the ministers. There must be a few humans somewhere to answer the telephone, and to deal with remonstrances from Iveagh House. (There too, there must be changes: the Secretary of that Department *must* be a horse). I think the first secretary of the new Irish legation should be a "lad"; thereafter a little establishment of jockeys, ostlers, stableman and trainers. The legation must be in the vicinity of broad parkland, where the Minister can take morning exercise prior to his breakfast of duty-free oats. Thereafter he should be encouraged to recline in a really decent stable.[112]

More recently a niche has been found in the health sector: horses are being used for healing mental and physical disabilities in human beings. The movement of the horse affects a rider's posture, balance, coordination and sensorimotor systems. Horses can also become emotional mirrors for human beings. They respond to the feeling state we show. Being herd and prey animals, they have a strong emotional sense which they have used for centuries as a survival tool. They feed off of and respond to other horses in the herd. They carry this natural and encoded empathy in their encounters with us.

The answer, however, is not to find some petty utilitarian purpose for our horses to allow them breathing space to survive in our midst. The imperative for us is to forget all about what a horse can do, and set about discovering what horses really are in themselves before they ever wear a saddle on their back or a bridle in their mouth. To see, smell, touch, mount a horse in the flesh is to feel the stirrings of energies dating from at least 35,000 years of human contact with the horse.

....

112 I am indebted to my confrère John Columba McCann for retrieving this brainwave from bureaucratic oblivion. Neither of us have any idea where this text can be found in printed form.

When I was eleven years of age, spending the summer on my grandparents' estate, I used, as often as I could do it unobserved, to steal into the stable and gently stroke the neck of my darling - a broad dapple-grey horse. It was not a casual delight but a great, certainly friendly, but also deeply stirring happening. If I am to explain it now, beginning from the still very fresh memory of my hand, I must say that what I experienced in touch with the animal was the Other, the immense otherness of the Other, which, however, did not remain strange like the otherness of the ox and the ram, but rather let me draw near and touch it. When I stroked the mighty mane, sometimes marvellously smooth-combed, at other times just as astonishingly wild, and felt the life beneath my hand, it was as though the element of vitality itself bordered on my skin, something that was not I, was certainly not akin to me, palpably the other, not just another, really the Other itself; and yet it let me approach, confided itself to me, placed itself elementally in the relation of Thou and Thou with me. The horse, even when I had not begun by pouring oats for him into the manger, very gently raised his massive head, ears flicking, then snorted quietly, as a conspirator gives a signal meant to be recognisable only by his fellow-conspirator; and I was approved.[113]

That we no longer need horses for travel, work on the farm or transport of goods, doesn't mean that horses have outlived their welcome. Finding new uses for them in the entertainment or therapeutic world is not necessary to give them the right to exist. We must look for and find something more essential. Finding what's invisible in the horse, the essence of what they are in themselves, requires that we cease to value and measure them according to what they can do for us. In one of the shortest poems he ever wrote, D.H. Lawrence describes such an encounter:

....

113 Martin Buber, *Between Man and Man*, Fontana, London, 1961, p. 11.

The youth walks up to the white horse, to put its halter on
and the horse looks at him in silence.
They are so silent, they are in another world.[114]

Most children in our culture have no experience of such hands-on
connection with a horse. Urban children become familiar with the horse
mainly through folk and fairy tales, movies and television. For them, only
a mythical relationship to horses is possible. When the horse enters our
dreams, magical qualities emerge whether or not we are currently aware
of any waking reality. Most folk tales portray the horse as an extension of
the physical abilities of the rider. In our dreams we become centaurs and
horse becomes part of our life's adventure; literally and figuratively our
means of transport on a journey of self-discovery.

And if Freud is right, that dreams are to individuals what myths are
to societies, Celtic mythology has something to say about these ever-
recurring equine archetypes. The horse as 'Trickster' figure appears
constantly in Celtic folklore. Horses can become shape-shifting water
animals such as the Each Uisge or 'water horse,' corresponding to the
Scottish Kelpies. Typically these wear golden bridles that appeal to human
greed. Once we are on its back, the Kelpie dives to the bottom of the lake
or the ocean, figuratively suggesting the depths of the unconscious. In an
age of tractors, cars and mechanised farm machinery, horse whisperings
spread through mass media to people, especially children, who have had
little or no contact with a live horse. Old movies such as *National Velvet*
and *Black Beauty*, conspire with newer ones like *Seabiscuit* and *Hidalgo* to
provide extensions of archetypal imagery to a newer generation.

War Horse (1982), the British novel by Michael Morpurgo captured
the imagination of a wide readership as it tried to convey the experience
of recent warfare through the eyes of a horse. 'Black Beauty goes to war,'
one critic dubbed it. The novel describes the experiences of Joey, a horse

---

114 'The White Horse' from *The Complete Poems of D.H. Lawrence*, Collected and Edited by
Vivian De Sola Pinto and Warren Roberts, Volume Two, London, Heinemann, 1964, p. 683.

purchased in France by the British Army for service in World War I. Albert, son of the previous owner, tries to bring Joey safely home. The novel was turned into a play using life-size horse puppets in 2007. Eventually it became one of the top best films of 2011 with Steven Spielberg's cinematic presentation. While filming, fourteen different horses were used as the main horse character, eight of them portraying Joey as an adult animal, four as a colt and two as a foal. 'When I'm doing an Indy Movie, I'm watching Indiana Jones, not the horse he is riding,' said Spielberg, '... Suddenly I'm faced with the challenge of making a movie where I not only had to watch the horse, I had to compel the audience to watch it along with me. I had to pay attention to what it was doing and try to understand its feelings. It was a whole new experience for me.' Working with horses on this scale was a revelation for Spielberg: 'I was really amazed at how expressive horses are and how much they can show what they're feeling.'

In all three versions of the War Horse story, critics tried to identify its allurement: 'the joy lies in the skilled recreation of equine life and in the unshaken belief that humankind is ennobled by its love of the horse'.

In Greek mythology Pegasus was son of Medusa the Gorgon and Posseidon, God of the sea. The myth says that Pegasus was born as a winged horse because his father Poseidon had the shape of a horse when seducing Medusa. Whenever Pegasus was striking the side of a mountain with his hooves his marks caused springs to turn into flowing fountains of inspiration. Such springs became sacred to the Muses who loved and respected the 'flying horse'. One of those sacred springs was the Hippocrene (meaning 'horse spring') on Mt Helicon.

Pegasus
by Patrick Kavanagh

My soul was an old horse
Offered for sale in twenty fairs.
I offered him to the Church--the buyers

Were little men who feared his unusual airs.
One said: 'Let him remain unbid
In the wind and rain and hunger
Of sin and we will get him—
With the winkers thrown in--for nothing.'
Then the men of State looked at
What I'd brought for sale.
One minister, wondering if
Another horse-body would fit the tail
That he'd kept for sentiment
The relic of his own soul—
Said, 'I will graze him in lieu of his labour.'
I lent him for a week or more
And he came back a hurdle of bones,
Starved, overworked, in despair.
I nursed him on the roadside grass
To shape him for another fair.

I lowered my price. I stood him where
The broken-winded, spavined stand
And crooked shopkeepers said that he
Might do a season on the land –
But not for high-paid work in towns.
He'd do a tinker, possibly.
I begged, 'O make some offer now,
A soul is a poor man's tragedy.
He'll draw your dungiest cart,' I said,
'Show you short cuts to Mass,
Teach weather lore, at night collect
Bad debts from poor men's grass.'
And they would not.

Where the
Tinkers quarrel I went down
With my horse, my soul.
I cried, 'Who will bid me half a crown?'
From their rowdy bargaining
Not one turned. 'Soul,' I prayed,
'I have hawked you through the world
Of Church and State and meanest trade.
But this evening, halter off,
Never again will it go on.
On the south side of ditches
There is grazing of the sun.
No more haggling with the world....'

As I said these words he grew
Wings upon his back. Now I may ride him
Every land my imagination knew.[115]

Love your enemy, welcome the stranger, treat everyone as your equal; treat them as you would treat yourself. All this runs contrary to the 'natural' order where survival is for the fittest and value is attached to usefulness. We are inclined to offload the redundant and sacrifice the alien on the altar of the incumbent. Most tribes think of themselves as the chosen people, and see other tribes as less favoured by the gods. But even though our nature provides us with such tendencies, our genius and our specificity as human beings allow us to adjust ourselves to whatever standards of behaviour we choose to adopt. We are modifiable, adaptable and malleable, if we put our minds to it.

Whatever about the fox, the horses and the hounds, we have a definite choice in all such matters be they social, political, sporting or religious.

115 *Patrick Kavanagh, Collected Poems*, edited by Antoinette Quinn, London, Allen Lane, 1978, pp. 116-118.

Our DNA provides us with building blocks allowing us to construct our own completion. Nothing in the human world is inescapable or inevitable. Our behavioural makeup is not a blueprint encoded in our genes, it is the basic score for an unfinished symphony. We complete and finish ourselves through culture. We are responsible for the human beings we turn out to be. We are also responsible for the way we behave in, and the way we treat, the world around us and all the creatures in that world.

Pictures of a priest blessing a fox hunt in County Kilkenny caused apoplexy in the ICABS (Irish Council for the Abolition of Blood Sports) who called for a ban on all such paraliturgical lunacy. A statement from the Irish Catholic Bishops Conference of 2005 declared that this body 'does not condone the practice of priests blessing foxhunts'. ICABS felt some redress of balance when it was reported that Iarnród Éireann had run over some fox hounds which had strayed onto a railway track on the line from Waterford to Dublin. A spokesperson for Iarnród Éireann confirmed that a pack of hounds on the railway line just outside Mullinavat, Co. Kilkenny were struck by the 14.50pm train from Waterford to Dublin, that a number of dogs had been killed and that the train suffered a small amount of damage. The incident also caused the train to be delayed for a period of time. 'We would advise that no one should cross the railway line where there is not a designated crossing,' pleaded the spokesperson for Iarnród Éireann, adding that 'it is extremely dangerous.' Promoters of the drag-hunt indicated that their formula would have avoided all such collision.

Hillbilly existentialism

I happened to be born on this island, call it providence or happenstance, the name is irrelevant. God chose to reveal Godself to me on a particular mountain at a particular time in history. I am bearing witness to that epiphany. Whether you believe it or not means little to me. God will find any number of ways of approaching you. What I am proposing, however, is an explanation of this fact which amounts to elucidating a theology. What might seem entirely satisfactory to me would be of little use to anyone else unless it can establish itself as 'orthodox,' namely 'a right and just way' of worshipping God.

And I have spent a lifetime trying to square this personal epiphany with the Irish Roman Catholic theology into which I was born and baptised. More importantly, and more pressingly, the question boils down to this: where is 'God' to be found in the Ireland of today?

My subtitle 'Life as a Limerick' describes both the place and the manner of the investigation. A sense of humour is vital. No one has definitive answers to the questions I pose; each of us has both the privilege and the responsibility to answer for themselves the burning question of why it was that we were thrown onto this planet in a particular place at a particular time without our permission. And, if we publish such an account, we have, it seems to me, the duty towards others to make that attempted explanation as understandable and as readable as possible. There is always going to be a ludicrous aspect to our floundering attempts to explain the universe to ourselves and, therefore, we can make our ponderings less tedious if we admit this fact and highlight this dimension. I hope that what I have described as my 'life as a Limerick' will bring a smile to your face as well as a nod or two of agreement. A sense of humour can prompt a chuckle of collusion as it eases digestion and alleviates boredom.

Let me get three things clear before I go on to tell you what I really think about our present situation: Number one is that God has already saved the world without much help from us, and often in spite of the Church he supposedly founded to carry on the good work. Number two: God does not step away from the forms and structures that God has instituted; unless, and this is the great mystery of free will, unless we ourselves remove them from God.

They have forsaken me,
    the spring of living water,
and have dug their own cisterns,
    broken cisterns that cannot hold water.   (Jeremiah 2:13)

And number three: The Holy Spirit of God is with the Church of Jesus Christ until the end of time. The question is: are we with the Holy Spirit?

There is a famine in the land. People all over this country, and, indeed, further afield, are looking for spiritual sustenance. Most of the food troughs and irrigation systems, the spiritual infrastructure, are still in place, but nothing is coming through. In another few years these will have rusted, seized up; they will be no longer salvageable. The life of the Spirit risks being stifled through neglect. Arrangements for our spiritual nourishment were made in a simple though unusual way.

At the last supper, Jesus Christ, the God-Man, instigated a new culture, a new language, a new way of being alive on this earth, of 'being alive with what's invisible'. This originality and newness make it difficult to talk about the 'Eucharist' or find images to which it can be compared, alternative ways of expressing it. That is why it needs to be 'done' rather than described.

The Eucharist is an ontological reality: it changes our very being and concerns the deep structures of our planet and ourselves. We are talking about energising our lives from eternity, bursting through our space-time capsule by inserting the oxygen of infinity. Such new life is not just an addition to, or substitute for, our natural being, but it is a grafting or splicing which combines two 'natures' to effect a new creation, a relational metaphysics, a being as communion.

Ritual and liturgical expression of this mystery, which is always beyond our limited powers of comprehension, came long before theoretical explanation or dogmatic formulation. The truth of our strange yet very specific faith is this: not only can we make the 'real presence' of God happen now, but as we do so, we, in turn, become the body and blood of Christ, and the people around us who communicate with us, whether living or dead, in their turn, become the body and blood of Christ. We thereby all become one body through him, with him, and in him. We, all together, move (or are moved) into a new dimension, a new space-time warp, a new kind of unity. The fragments of creation which we hold in our hands are the security or bond of our deliverance. We hold on to these symbols for dear life. We need this medicine, this viaticum, this stimulant. Don't let anyone take it away from us, or persuade us that we don't need it, or that we are not worthy of it. Who could possibly be worthy? Worthiness is not a requirement.

Eucharist is a pick-me-up for the down-and-out, a panacea for the impaired, food for the feeble; it is not a booster for the already rehabilitated or a prize for the perfect. We need this sustenance, even more so if we are weak. This is, therefore, the most important act we can perform, so let's do it – let's fall *into* love, the love which the three persons of the Trinity live eternally together, with each other, which they exude and which radiates outwards from them to the ends of the earth.

Through this mystery we help transubstantiate our world into an immortal diamond. This happens little by little, stone by stone, as the walls of the Burren rise up out of fallen leaves. We help to transform or transfigure everything, beginning with ourselves, into the body and blood of Christ. By this means the economy of our ecology is transferred from ordinary biological necessity to the alternative energy of theological possibility. True religion should be the filter, by which, through which, and in which, divine love penetrates the universe.

Earth provides the grain which we mould into bread; vineyards offer fruit that crushes into wine. The ritual of thanksgiving instituted by Christ, which we call the Eucharist, is a unique technology to electrify the universe. This happens gradually and incrementally as long as we are prepared to offer ourselves as one thread in the overall tapestry, as one filament in the light bulb.

The elements used in such a transforming artistry were local and specific. These happened to be bread and wine because of cultural circumstances dictating the menu where the meal took place. Bread and wine were never meant to become the only and the unique elements in the divine equation, in the theological technology. The fetish we have developed around such random foodstuffs is laughable. Do we imagine that we would be left by God without the bread of life, which Jesus Christ came on earth to distribute to all those in need, because a priest was not available to distribute it or because some particular brand of flour or culture of grape was lacking?

An 11-year-old girl in Ohio with celiac disease received a gluten-free host which had been reserved on a special paten before the Mass took place. She wore a beaded cross made by her grandmother so the priest would know who she was. However, the director of the diocese insisted that Church law 'calls for the host to be wheat and wheat only'. Because Jesus ate wheat bread with his apostles before his Crucifixion, Church law requires the host to be wheat and only wheat, said the director of the Office for Divine Worship at the Diocese of Columbus. Without wheat, the wafers cannot be consecrated and used in Mass, so no gluten-free wafers.

In 1995, the Vatican said low-gluten hosts are valid if they hold enough gluten to make bread. Worshippers wanting the low-gluten option were required to present a medical certificate and obtain a bishop's approval. The policy was loosened in 2003 to eliminate the medical-certificate requirement and to allow pastors to grant approval.

U.S. Catholic bishops have approved two manufacturers of low-gluten wafers. One is the Benedictine Sisters of Perpetual Adoration in Missouri; the order's website says it has provided hosts for more than 2,000 celiac sufferers. The other is Parish Crossroads in Indiana, which provides low-gluten hosts made in Germany. The low-gluten wafers made by the Benedictine Sisters contain less than 100 parts per million, says a clinical dietitian at Nationwide Children's Hospital. She said the amount of gluten in one of the hosts is 0.004 milligrams and that researchers have found it takes about 10 milligrams per day to start a reaction. The U.S. Food and Drug Administration has proposed a rule that says products could be labelled gluten-free if the gluten content is less than 20 parts per million.

'Woe to you blind guides! You strain out a gnat but swallow a camel!' (Matthew 24:25).

That people who never drink wine and have never eaten bread, even more distressingly, that people who cannot drink wine and cannot eat bread, are required by law to import these products from countries who do so in order to have a valid Eucharist is as perverse as it is parochial.

Also, the elements which Christ used were meant to be physical, cultural, material elements, in keeping with the principles of incarnation. The way in which we have tried to remove their physicality, their materiality, by turning the bread into barely visible or tangible hosts to feed the angels (*Panis Angelicus*) so that it can melt on your tongue without any effort to chew; this is yet one more result of our heretical urge towards bloodless refinement. Nor should it matter which particular elements are used, the reality is that Christ has become incarnate in our natural world and heretofore every aspect of that created world is potentially part of his body and blood until Christ becomes all in all.

Teilhard de Chardin, palaeontologist and priest, more than once found himself in remote areas of the world without any church building, formal altar, paten and chalice, bread and wine, or any congregation. These experiences led him to create 'The Mass on the World,' where he used the desert as his table and the people of the world as his bread and wine. In his book, *Hymn of the Universe*, he records the eucharistic liturgy he created for such occasions. The 'whole earth' becomes his altar. The 'depths of a soul laid widely open to all the forces which in a moment will rise up from every corner of the earth and converge upon the Spirit' become his paten and chalice. He places the earth's harvest on this paten and fills this chalice with 'all the sap which is to be pressed out this day from the earth's fruits'.

To interpret adequately the fundamental position of the Eucharist in the economy of the world ... it is, I think, necessary that Christian thought and Christian prayer should give great importance to the real and physical extensions of the Eucharistic Presence ... As we properly use the term 'our bodies' to signify the localised centre of our spiritual radiations ..., so it must be said that in its initial and primary meaning the term 'Body of Christ' is limited, in this context, to the consecrated species of Bread and Wine. But ... the host is comparable to a blazing fire whose flames spread out like rays all round it ... Beneath the inertness of the morsel of bread a consuming power which, far from being absorbed into me, absorbs me into itself ... The essential vocation of the world is to attain completion, through a chosen part of its whole being, in the plenitude of the incarnate Word.[116]

Through our participation, and through the material elements chosen for the consecration, the universe takes on the lineaments of Jesus Christ, and is caused to rise by the power of this yeast until it becomes one loaf. This happens slowly but incrementally each time we incorporate ourselves into the body of Christ. The Eucharist is essentially the symbol of unity. Unity as a hallmark is even more important than truth or beauty or goodness. It should be the most telling characteristic of the one true church of Jesus Christ, more than holiness, more than catholicity (meaning universality) more than derivation from the apostles. Unity is *the* defining hallmark.

Vatican Council II supports this assertion: 'In the celebration of the Eucharist is found the high point both of the action by which God sanctifies the world in Christ and of the worship that the human race offers to the father, adoring him through Christ the Son of God, in the Holy Spirit.' For this reason, 'the entire celebration is planned in such a way that it leads to a conscious, active, and full participation of the faithful both in body and in mind, a participation burning with faith, hope and charity, of the sort which is desired by the Church and demanded by the very nature of the celebration, and to which the

....
116 Teilhard de Chardin, *Hymn of the Universe*, Collins, London, 1965, pp. 13-15; 148-152.

Christian people have a right and duty by reason of their Baptism.'[117] This last line could be understood as saying that a priest is ordained to serve the priesthood of the faithful.

'Every valley shall be exalted, and every mountain and hill shall be made low. The uneven shall be made level, and the rough places a plain' (Isaiah 40:4). There are 'hills of truth' all over the world. This does not mean 'pantheism,' or belief that God is nature, that God is Knockfierna. It does mean 'panentheism'; that God is 'in' everything and is everywhere present in the nature which God created.

What Seamus Heaney's poetry attempts to reveal is that, 'all of life is potentially vivid with advent, with the things of the world placed against the relief of an infinite field of vision'.[118] There may be Knockfiernas or 'hills of truth' all over the world, but Ireland is God-bespattered, specifically pockmarked with such places and we have evidence of people finding such truth all over this island for the last 6,000 years at least. From the Skellig Islands at the tip of our southern sea coast to the Giants' Causeway in the furthest northern outreach, this island is loaded with sacred places where millions have triggered adumbrations. Like Alexander's horse, we have to be turned away from our shadows and shown how to start from scratch.

Knockfierna is not just pre-Celtic, pre-Christian, pre-Historic, it is pre-personal. It was there as a reality before any human eye could see. Before any evolutionary eyeball popped its socket in the animal or even the insect world, this cheeky protuberance on the earth's surface, cone of an extinct volcano perhaps, had found its form. The natural world which has graced this site from the beginning of time is well used to sharing with human dwellers. We have evidence of human habitation going back some considerable time. But what are six thousand or even fifty thousand years in terms of those millions through which rock formations have presided, hosting trees, birds, insects, animals and open skies long before we ever

117 *General Instruction of the Roman Missal*, n.16 & 18.
118 Daniel Tobin, *Passage to the Center*, University Press of Kentucky, 1999, p. 259.

came on the scene. Since the human family arrived, each generation has written a story in ways that allow us to recreate the history of how the human population has behaved in such a place. We might even congratulate ourselves that the relationship here has been more or less benign up to now. Compared with other places in the world which have been exploited or destroyed by careless or cutthroat human habitation, Knockfierna has remained more or less intact. Apart from some hideous paraphernalia for boosting radio or TV signals, which, hopefully, the mountain can shake off its shoulder like howdahs from an elephant or a camel's back, plus, of course, the thirteen foot cement cross erected in 1950, the terrain has remained recognisably similar in outline to what it always was.

Some of this inaction is owing to lack of interest. The site has never been much of a money spinner: there are no oil wells or gold mines to exploit. However, with the comparatively recent development of the tourist industry, and Ireland's discovery of this as one of the most potent earners for our fragile economy, the demise of Knockfierna as we know it today, and have known it for centuries, could be imminent. A tarmacadam road to the top, even with the laudable aim of providing wheelchair access, would constitute a sure-fire way of driving Donn Fíreannach right out of his *Poll na Bruíne*.

Knockfierna and so many other somewhat secret places in Ireland must be allowed to develop their own way of welcoming the stranger. Tourism Ireland has undertaken a world-class marketing campaign with an aggressive seduction strategy towards 23 markets across the globe. A 2019 global greening campaign became the highlight of such promotion. 'Going Green for St Patrick is a great way to get the world talking about Ireland,' the tourist trumpeters bellow: 'It's a simple idea with minimal costs, but it's also an incredibly effective marketing strategy. It gets Ireland on to front pages around the world, at a time of year when people are planning their summer breaks.' Last year St Patrick's page received more than 425,000 views on March 17, about 150 times more than normal. Once a year, the apostle of Ireland is a Wikipedia celebrity.

The Taj Mahal, the Niagara Falls, the Leaning Tower of Pisa, the Empire State Building; go green to celebrate Saint Patrick. In Chicago the river running through the city goes green to start a weekend of celebrations. 'The idea of dyeing the Chicago River green,' says Bill King, erstwhile co-ordinator of St Patrick Celebrations in Chicago, 'originally came about by accident when plumbers were cleaning the sewers and using fluorescein dye to trace illegal substances that were polluting the river.' Ironically, the dye itself is orange. But once it hits the water, it becomes bright emerald.

Before the nineteenth century, relatively wild, remote areas were not seen as beautiful but as uncivilised and dangerous. In 1725 Daniel Defoe of *Robinson Crusoe* fame described areas which today are prime tourist venues as 'the most desolate, wild and abandoned country in all England'. Before the nineteenth century, for instance, Scotland was a barbarous jungle visited only by adventurers and sportspeople, until Queen Victoria looked out the window of her carriage on a summer visit and delighted in what she saw. Suddenly the stamp of royal approval upon 'the Queen's view' turned the spot into one of the major tourist venues in the world.

And this only because ordinary people began to have leisure and money enough to travel and to transform themselves from troglodytes into tourists. Transport improved beyond recognition. Hotels were built to accommodate the crowds of visitors. Some of these now fly from the other end of the world to relish this scenery and avail of these luxuries.

It was poetry that changed our view: Wordsworth and the Romantic Poets created a whole climate of mysticism around natural beauty and the aura of the countryside which most of us take for granted today.

Once again I see
These hedge-rows, hardly hedge-rows, little lines
Of sportive wood run wild: these pastoral farms,
Green to the very door; and wreaths of smoke
Sent up, in silence, from among the trees!

I cannot paint
What then I was. The sounding cataract
Haunted me like a passion: the tall rock,
The mountain, and the deep and gloomy wood,
Their colours and their forms, were then to me
An appetite; a feeling and a love . . .
Therefore am I still
A lover of the meadows and the woods,
And mountains; and of all that we behold
From this green earth; of all the mighty world
Of eye and ear; . . . well pleased to recognise
In nature and the language of the sense,
The anchor of my purest thoughts, the nurse,
The guide, the guardian of my heart, and soul
Of all my moral being.[119]

When *Star Wars* was filmed on the Skelligs in 2014, thousands of fans, dressed as Darth Vadar and Chewbacca, flocked to the island. Should we know beforehand what we want to be and to see when we visit such places? Do we visit the Skelligs to watch star wars and do we come there as who we are or as a stand in for Luke Skywalker? Who cares if it fills the coffers of local business? Portmagee was transformed by the interest generated. Can 'the Force' awaken in Ballingarry? The question is simply this: does Knockfierna want a piece of this potential pie? If so, it better shape up or ship out.

There are many entrepreneurs and developers who could, as they see it, put things right. A Disneyland playground, with MacDonald's in tow plus a few Pizza Huts scattered around the hillside would solve your immediate food problems; a 'Knock-the-Rock –Fierna Festival' with sexy brochure advertising rock concerts featuring well-known Irish and foreign bands would

119 William Wordsworth, from 'Lines Composed above Tintern Abbey', *Poems of Wordsworth*, Chosen and Edited by Matthew Arnold, London, Macmillan, 1947, p. 250.

up the ante and get things going. Streamlined travel systems connecting local airports and train stations, with multipurpose accommodation sprouting along the highway could turn Knockfierna into Limerick's Las Vegas. All we need, they tell us, is the right kind of leadership, the appropriate injection of capital, and strong investment from local business.

Fortunately, accidents of history and circumstance have preserved this sanctuary from well-meaning promoters who see it as Jurassic Park. A few dinosaur heads peeping out from *Poll na Bruíne* and you're on your way and so are the crowds.

This is the quandary which faces us all over the country. How to maintain the balance between viability and insolvency; between welcoming visitors and being overrun by them; between providing access to the site and destroying the magic of the place.

There are places on this planet where the unsuspecting tourist can be ambushed, like Eurydice, and carried to another world. We can so easily overlook or neglect what can only be described as our sacred places. Human beings and, indeed, nature itself, have used this as a place of worship for thousands of years. This does not mean appropriation by any particular religion or denomination. People who come, whether by accident or design, repeat to those who meet them: 'I don't know what I believe, or if I believe in anything, but when I am here, when I visit this place something happens to me, quite without my permission or my intention, and I am touched by something outside of myself, touched to the heart.' Such places are dotted around this country and need to be guarded, sheltered, preserved.

Sea, sky and countryside provide a living stage for mythological manoeuvrings which have happened and been recorded since humans first inhabited these places. Earth, fire, air and water, the elements of our world can become 'zig-zag hieroglyphs for life itself'. Artists of every kind have recognised and represented these dimensions in ways that provide an all-embracing psychic memory now embedded in the rocks. Their 'embroidered cloths' are maps which show what no ordnance survey or satellite picture can depict. Every vista in every province is potentially an opening to such an alternative world.

Those of us living on this island of Ireland could revive the secret ways in which our ancestors aligned themselves with natural cycles and eternal dimensions. These offer at least some of our specific dignity as human beings. Ireland, along with Greece and the Scandinavian countries could provide a haven for this aspect of our humanity. We could become for Europe, and for the world, an oasis in a desert of unilateral thinking. Ireland could be a sanctuary providing a natural landscape for those wishing to taste and see and hear an alternative reality, not just for antiquarian or tourist delectation, but as essential 'dreamtime' for anyone hoping to live a fully integrated and comprehensive human life.

> I have spread my dreams under your feet;
> Tread softly because you tread on my dreams.[120]

Our island is small and self-contained enough to provide an object lesson and a case history of mythological landscape. Every acre of each province is a geography of lived folklore, of consecrated ground. Holy mountains, sacred hills, fairy forts, ancient trees and healing wells are to be found in settings second to none in terms of natural beauty. Poets and prophets have known this reality. Elizabeth Barret Browning said, 'Earth's crammed with heaven, and every common bush afire with God'. In the poem 'God's Grandeur' Gerard Manley Hopkins, who spent time in Ireland, sees that 'The world is charged with the grandeur of God'.

> It will flame out like shining from shook foil;
> It gathers to a greatness, like the ooze of oil
> Crushed.

----

120 W.B. Yeats, 'He wishes for the Cloths of Heaven'.

Patrick Kavanagh knows that 'Christ comes with a January flower'.

Christianity believes in the miracle of creation and the mystery of incarnation. These two mysteries conspire to suggest that every inch of space and every moment of time are possibilities of revelation. In other words, each moment and each fragment are potentially sacraments. Those who insist that there are only seven sacraments, and that they are personally in charge of these, with complete control over their dispensation and distribution are windmills who think they cause the wind. But 'the wind blows where it will. You hear its sound, but you cannot tell where it comes from or where it is going' (John 3:8).

When I was studying with Yves Congar at Le Saulchoir in Paris in the 1960s, he suggested that the Church only stretched its theology when forced to do so in extreme instances. During the Crusades knights who were dying by themselves on mountainsides would give themselves communion by saying the words of consecration over three blades of grass or the leaves from a tree or whatever natural element was within reach.

I later found an article in *The Dublin Review* of 1897 by Walter Sylvester which describes 'The Communions with Three Blades of Grass of the Knights Errant'. This article provides a number of examples from the literature of the Middle Ages suggesting that such was the common practice of the time.

As for the Sacrament of Confession, in 1349, during the plague known as The Black Death, lay confession was practised in Somersetshire by the express direction of the bishop of the diocese. So terrible had been the effect of the scourge among the clergy of Somerset that, as early as 17th January, 1349, the Bishop of Bath and Wells felt himself constrained to address a letter of advice to his flock:

> The contagious nature of the present pestilence, which is ever spreading itself far and wide, has left many parish churches and other cures, and consequently the people of our diocese, destitute of curates and priests. And inasmuch as priests cannot be found ...

we urgently enjoin upon you and command you ... that *in articulo mortis*, if they are not able to obtain any priest, they should make confession of their sins (according to the teaching of the apostle) even to a layman, and, if a man is not at hand, to a woman.

How different from the attitude today. Cardinal Mauro Piacenza, head of the Apostolic Penitentiary has said even though the world is facing a pandemic that may limit many people's ability to celebrate the sacraments, particularly those people who are in isolation, quarantining or hospitalised with Covid-19, confession by phone is still most likely invalid.

In an interview on 5th December, 2020 with the Vatican newspaper, *L'Osservatore Romano*, the cardinal was asked whether a phone or other electronic means of communication could be used for confession.

'We can confirm the probable invalidity of the absolution imparted through such means,' he said. 'In fact, the real presence of the penitent is lacking, and there is no real conveyance of the words of absolution; there are only electric vibrations that reproduce the human word.'

Is it not true that confession right into the ear of a priest sitting beside you is a matter of electric vibration no matter how you choose to interpret it? The eardrum vibrates from the incoming sound waves of your articulated sentences and his reverberating eardrum sends these vibrations to his middle ear. The bones in his middle ear increase the sound vibrations and send them to the cochlea, a snail-shaped structure filled with fluid in the middle ear. Here chemicals create an electrical signal which the auditory nerve carries to his brain. So, only electric vibrations can carry a human word from one real human person to another in any circumstances..

Get a life Cardinal Mauro Piacenza because in the end 'everything in life is vibration,' as Einstein says.

More books from the Author

Living the Mystery

(COLUMBA BOOKS, HARDBACK, €19.99) ISBN: 9781782183563

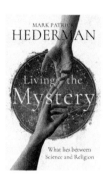

The world has never been more in need of religion. The lack of it is destroying us in so many ways. A false argument between science and scripture needs to be diverted. Religion has its own reasons, its own language, its own access to truth. Unless we learn this language and sing this song we risk losing our most precious heritage. Mark Patrick Hederman has lived as a Benedictine monk for over fifty years. This life has taught him how to engage with mystery. In this book he tries to explain as simply as he can how to bring religion back into your life.

The Opal and the Pearl

(COLUMBA BOOKS, HARDBACK, €19.99) ISBN: 9781782183068

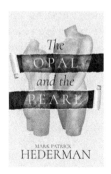

With seven billion human beings on one planet we need a new ethics guiding us in our way of relating to one another sexually. Author Mark Patrick Hederman critiques Catholic teaching on sex, and stresses the need for an ethics of sexual behavior outside the very specific and particular demands of heterosexual marriage. The message of artists has been consistent: 'we cannot be reduced to any formula. We have to accept the blood-and-guts reality of what we are. We need to be human, fully human and any ethics must provide for us as such.'

All books are available to order directly from www.columbabooks.com

More books from the Author

Underground Cathedrals

(COLUMBA BOOKS, PAPERBACK, €14.99) ISBN: 9781856076951

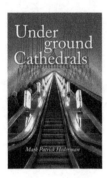

'My proposal is that, at this time, the Holy Spirit is unearthing an underground cathedral in Ireland which could help to replace the pretentious, over-elaborate Irish Catholic architecture of the twentieth century.'
Coupled with very incisive and honest comments on the current state of the church, and with a reflective meditation on the Murphy Report on the Dublin Archdiocese, Abbot Hederman offers a visionary and very stimulating image of how things might be if only we all listen to the voices of artists in our midst.

Dancing with Dinosaurs

(COLUMBA BOOKS, PAPERBACK, €9.99) ISBN: 9781856077354

Dinosaurs have been described as the most successful animals that ever inhabited this planet. We had to learn how to live with them, and survive in spite of them. Today we have invented our own dinosaurs. Churches, banks and multinationals are some of the modern breed of dinosaur. Small may be beautiful, but in the world in which we live it is not very durable. Unless any organisation becomes a dinosaur it will not survive the vicissitudes of history.

All books are available to order directly from www.columbabooks.com